THE BOOK OF
SQUASH

To
George Cummings
and
John Greco

THE BOOK OF
SQUASH

PETER WOOD

Series Editor: James Wagenvoord

LITTLE, BROWN AND COMPANY

Boston　　　　　　　　Toronto

C

Photographs by James Wagenvoord, unless otherwise indicated
Designed by Anita Wagenvoord
Published by arrangement with Van Nostrand Reinhold

Library of Congress Cataloging in Publication Data

Wood, Peter, 1930-
    The book of squash.

    Reprint of the ed. published by Van Nostrand Reinhold,
New York.
    1. Squash rackets (Game) I. Title.
GV1004.W66 1974   796.34'3   74-8530
ISBN 0-316-95160-9

Published simultaneously in Canada
by Little, Brown & Company (Canada) Limited

Printed in The United States of America

ACKNOWLEDGMENTS

● The author extends warms thanks to W. Stewart Brauns Jr., former President of the United States Squash Racquets Association, for aid on many historical points in this book; to Robert Lehman for the same help and for access to his vast archives of squash photographs; to Benjamin Swett for his photographs; to Fred Weymuller, president of the Professional Association, for pointing them out to me and for other assistance; to the USSRA for permission to reprint the American rules of squash racquets; to the editors of the *New York Times Sunday Magazine* in general and to William Honan in particular for help in preparing the material on the Ufford-Adair match, which appeared as an article under their cover; and finally to an ever-agreeable opponent, Ramsay W. Vehslage, for appearing in the court with me long enough for Jim Wagenvoord to catch on film many of the book's illustrative if not always exemplary action sequences.

CONTENTS

GLOSSARY

BOAST — A three-wall shot that caroms into either of the front corners. Most often hit off the backhand.

CENTER SERVICE LINE — The line perpendicular to the back wall dividing the service area into left and right rectangles.

COMING AROUND — Words used to alert an opponent that a player is *turning on the ball*. Often a player will merely shout "turning!" or "around!" The cry warns the opponent to get out of the way.

CORNER SHOT — A ball hit tightly into either front corner, hitting the side wall first, then the front wall.

CROSS-COURT — A shot hit in a deep V from one side of the court to the other.

DIE — When a ball fails to bounce enough to be returned.

DOUBLES — Squash racquets played in a larger court than singles (45′ x 25′) with two players on a side.

DOWN THE LINE — Hugging one of the side walls. A ball so hit is often called an alley shot or a rail shot.

DRIVE — A hard-hit ball.

DROP SHOT — A ball hit softly so that it makes its second bounce close to the front wall.

FAULT — A bad serve.

GALLERY — An area to accommodate spectators.

GET — A return of a difficult shot.

HALF-VOLLEY — A ball hit on the rise just after it bounces.

LET — A point to be played over. *See rules.*

LET POINT — A point awarded to a player when his opponent interferes with him illegally. *See rules.*

LOB — A ball hit in a high looping arc.

NICK — A ball that hits the juncture of a wall and floor so that it rolls out without bouncing. An automatic winner.

NO SET — A game played to the standard 15 points after having been tied at 13 or 14 all. *See rules.*

PUTAWAY — A shot that cannot be retrieved; a winner.

RAIL SHOT — A shot hit *down the line;* an alley shot.

RALLY — A prolonged series of shots and returns.

REVERSE CORNER — A *corner shot* hit from the opposite side of the court.

SERVICE BOX — The quarter circle marked in the left and right service areas. A server must keep one foot in the service box while serving.

SERVICE QUARTER CIRCLE — Same as *service box.*

SERVICE LINE — Both the line on the front wall above which the serve must hit, and the line parallel to the front wall on the floor demarking the service area.

T — The strategic center of the court, where the service line and the center service line form a T.

TELLTALE — The 17-inch-high strip of metal across the front wall that resounds when hit with the ball.

TIN — Slang for *telltale.*

TOUCH — The ability of a player to hit the ball precisely where and how he desires.

TURNING ON THE BALL — Following a ball around the back wall by turning bodily with it. For example, a player standing in the right half of the court preparing to return a shot that is coming off the right wall may hit it directly with his forehand or he may turn with it as it proceeds to bounce off the floor and the back wall and then hit it with his backhand.

VOLLEY — A ball hit before it bounces.

WINNER — A putaway.

AN·INTRODUCTION
TO THE GAME

CONFESSIONS OF AN ENTHUSIAST

● Books about sports are traditionally authored by experts, like Jack Nicklaus on golf or Pancho Gonzales on tennis. This book is about squash racquets, to give the sport its full name — what it is, how it got that way, and how it is played in America. But most of all, it is about the zest of the game, and in that one important respect it follows tradition: it is written by an expert. There are hundreds of players better at squash than I am, but only a few who take more pleasure in the game — and they, I have always suspected, are nuts.

Like most players today, I first saw squash played as a college freshman. The place was Hamilton, a small liberal-arts college for men in upstate New York. Tucked away in the then-new gymnasium, between the glossy basketball court and the glass-walled swimming pool, almost as an afterthought on the part of the architect, were four fine courts. Hamilton had no squash team back in 1948, and aside from their use in the college's compulsory physical education program, the courts were often idle. This, I am told, is no longer true.

As I toured the gymnasium that first day, what I saw from the squash gallery — really little more than a corridor that overlooked the courts from above the rear wall — were four rectangular, gleaming white pits, with no windows and apparently no doors. One of them was brightly lit by fixtures recessed in the ceiling, and in it two racquet-wielding men in gym suits and sneakers were running wildly to and fro, whacking a little black ball around the walls with infectious gusto. The first question that came to my mechanistic mind was how they had gotten in. Then I spotted the small access door set flush, hardware and all, into the rear wall of the court. It gave, I later learned, onto a corridor that ran underneath the gallery. Each door was fitted with a small square of thick glass that allowed someone outside to peep inside to see whether the court was occupied and by whom.

An angular pattern of red lines overlaid the white walls and floor. Attached to the front wall a foot or so above the floor ran a narrow strip of sheet metal, its top edge beveled at a 45-degree angle and painted red. When one of the players hit it with the hard rubber ball, it produced a loud clang and play stopped. Clearly, it acted as a sort of net, if one were to compare the game to tennis or badminton. For a ball to be good, apparently, it had to hit the front wall above the telltale, as I later learned this metal strip is called.

Equally obvious was the fact that the two men down in the court flailing away with sturdy badminton-sized racquets were taking turns hitting the ball — or missing it, as the level of squash at Hamilton was none too high in those days.

I also noted (although I did not fully appreciate its significance at the time) the third essential of the game, the feature that more than any other gives squash its especially broad appeal and makes it fun to play at any level and very easy to pick up. Even when the ball was hit too hard or too high or at the wrong angle, as it usually was by the two players I was watching, it rarely went out of bounds, as it would have in tennis or any other open-court game. (The relatively new game of paddle tennis, played outdoors on duckboards in a chicken-wire enclosure, has something of the same advantage, accounting for its great and growing popularity in suburbia.) Play continued until one of the men actually missed the ball entirely or failed to get it to the front wall above the telltale. Morover, because the ball could be taken off the side and back walls, even when it was driven past one of the players he often had a second chance at it. What this meant was an enormous amount of exercise in a very short period of time and in a relatively small space. Already the two players below me were perspiring through their sweatshirts.

Fascinated, I watched to the end. Within ten minutes after my arrival both men, puffing mightily, had had enough and made their exit through the little door in the rear of the court. A second later the lights went out, but it was too late; I was hooked.

Since then, I have played on and off for more than two decades, and my experience, probably as much as anyone else's, illustrates the pitfalls and pleasures that lie ahead for the average player who takes up squash. What lies ahead for the champion is the subject of a future chapter.

I learned the game in a haphazard way at Hamilton, where there was no one of caliber to play with and no coach. This in no way diminished the pleasure I took in the game at the time, but it did start me off with bad habits that I carry with me today. It makes good sense for anyone taking up the game to arrange for lessons if possible, so that he will have the basics to work on. One of the nice things about squash is that a person can practice it by himself, alone in the court, without having to worry about boring someone across the net from him. Unfortunately, squash is so much fun to play that most players neglect this solitary practice, which could improve their game immensely.

After Hamilton there was a brief stint at Newport, R.I., where I was stationed while in the navy. My first concentrated play, however, came during a winter I spent as a student in Paris, living on the G.I. Bill. The tiny *chambre de bonne* that I rented on the top floor of an old eight-story apartment house near the Etoile not only had no elevator, it had no running water. To my great pleasure I discovered that just a few blocks from where I lived stood the shabby old Jeu de Paum, where one of two formerly elegant court-tennis courts (*jeu de paum* in French) had been converted into three squash courts. The exercise was welcome, but more important from my standpoint were the showers. In order to bathe and shave, I played squash nearly every day.

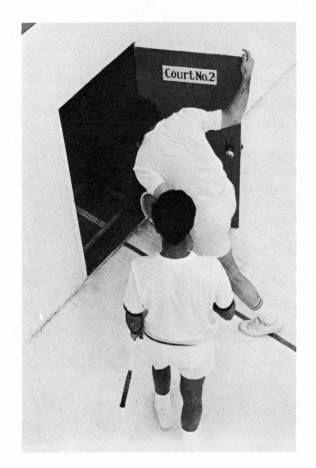

Throughout Europe and most of the rest of the world the British game is played. The court is two feet wider than ours, and the ball is softer and slower, which means the player must move to it rather than let the ball come to him. I have heard the British game described by its enthusiasts as being far superior to the American game because it requires a greater repertoire of shots. On the other hand, one British player of note recently described his national version of the game as about the equivalent of "whacking a dead mouse around the court with a wet mop." In either case it requires that you run, and I learned to run that winter, a facility that does not need special instruction and still remains the strong point of my game.

Finally, and presently, I have played in New York City. About a dozen years ago, while living in semi-squalor on the Lower East Side, I scraped together the dues and the recommendations necessary to join the University Club, not an easy feat for a beginning writer with only one presentable suit. However, I felt the cost could be deducted

from the future medical and psychiatric bills I would otherwise be paying to maintain my atrophying body and soothe my frustrated aggressive instincts. It has turned out to be by far the wisest investment I have ever made, either of time or of money. And I wonder how it is possible for other, seemingly normal people to exist amid the choking urban coagulation without regularly stretching their muscles in some competitive way.

In short order I found myself involved in league play — at the bottom of the Club's C League team with the old-world professional George Cummings, since retired, making wry comments on my form. At the time, this was indeed starting at the bottom (there is now a D League in the metropolitan New York area, which means that players just starting the game can find formal competition to egg them on). It has been uphill ever since, and as invigorating and enjoyable a climb as ever there was. I shall not reach the very top, but I can play with those who have, and the view is vast. My one regret is that I took no formal instruction at the beginning, which leaves me with bad habits and a lack of confidence in my strokes. Although I know better and can suggest better, these failings inevitably surface at the most crucial moments in tight matches and doom me forever to a rank below the top A League players.

At forty, I still play as much as ever — averaging three times a week during the competitive season (November through April) and nearly as often during the rest of the year, because I don't play tennis, not by choice or to maintain the purity of my squash stroke, but simply because I have no easy access to any tennis courts. There is a persistent myth, incidentally, that squash hurts one's tennis game, the strokes being so different. In fact, the two sports complement each other marvelously. Both require the hand-eye coordination that is the *sine qua non* of playing racquet sports well. Squash trains one's reflexes and wind, while tennis builds power, concentration, and pinpoint accuracy.

The main factor that keeps me and thousands like me playing competitive squash, rather than simply using the game to keep my waistline within bounds, is that I have, or at least I think I have (which in this case is the same thing), improved slightly each year. True, this is possible only because I started from such a low base. The top-flight players — those who played competitive squash in prep school and college, were coached in the basic strokes from the beginning, and mastered the game at an early age — normally reach their peak during their twenties or early thirties. It is harder for them to keep up the fevered pitch of competitive play when they recognize that they are not the players they once were.

However, there are certain inducements to keep the competitive spirit of good players alive. Chief among them is the intriguing game of doubles, which requires more tactical skill and less blind speed than singles and can therefore be played at championship level much longer. There are also special tournaments for players over forty, called Veterans, and for those over fifty, called Seniors. Halfway through my squash career, I have all that to look forward to.

THE
SQUASH
COURT

What I had to look forward to twenty-two years ago at Hamilton was the translation of my first impressions of the game into hard facts. I doubt if there is one squash player in a hundred who can tell you off the top of his head the exact dimensions of the court he has spent hundreds of hours in. I certainly could not. But I have looked them up. The Hamilton courts were regulation-size (not all, by any means, are). So what I was seeing over the gallery rail was a room with a floor 32 feet long and 18½ feet wide. Those dimensions, incidentally, were arrived at back in 1924, when the newborn U.S. Squash Racquets Association sought to standardize the game. Until

that time, courts were built in a bewildering variety of sizes, usually dictated by the space available. The USSRA simply took note of the various lengths and widths of the courts then existing in this country — there were not many — worked out the mathematical average, rounded off the figures, and came up with 32 by 18½. They determined the height of the walls (which I will come to later) the same way. When the British, four years later, decided to formalize their game, they performed the same arithmetic, but because they were working from a different set of statistics, they naturally came up with different dimensions — 32 feet long and 21 feet wide.

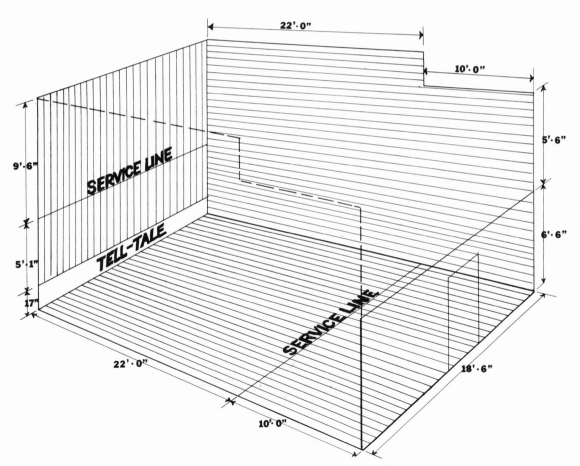

Historians of the game can give a less precise explanation for why the American and English balls differ so much. The best reason seems to be that the games developed like separate dialects of the same language at a time before jet travel had shrunk the world to its present size. Evidence of how this can happen is that in Australia today, where they still play according to British rules and in the British-sized court, the favored ball is considerably faster than that used in England. Those who are working for a standard that will make international competition possible — a sort of squash Esperanto, if you will — are looking with favor on this Australian ball as a step toward compromise.

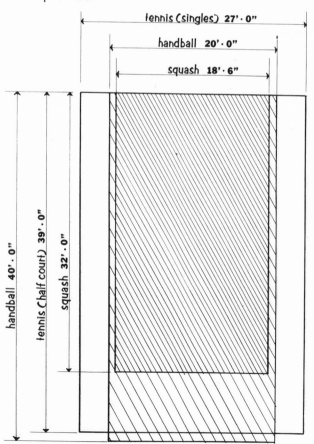

The dimensions of the American court make it 9 feet shorter and 8½ feet narrower than one side of a tennis court. To follow play, it may help to imagine a squash court as actually being a tennis court folded back on itself, Alice-in-Wonderland style, with the metal telltale, its beveled top 17 inches above the floor, being the net. A rebound off the 16-foot-high front wall above the telltale would be, then, equivalent to a tennis ball clearing the net and passing into the opposite court. At that point the court becomes the exclusive property of the receiving player, who is burdened with returning the ball to the front wall (over the net), either taking it on the fly (a tennis volley) or after it has bounced no more than once on the floor. While he is attempting to do so, his opponent must keep out of his way.

Simple. But now add to that picture two side walls with playing surfaces the same height as the front wall for most of their length but stepped down to 12 feet toward the rear of the court; a back wall with a playing surface 6½ feet high; and the provision that on its journey to or from the front wall the ball may be caromed off any or all of the other walls in the room (in squash, unlike four-wall handball, the ceiling is out of bounds), and you have the game of squash in a nutshell — or if not exactly in a nutshell, at least in a lidless wooden box.

Ideally, the inner floor and walls of this box are lined with more than 2,000 inch-thick lengths of kiln-dried, clear, tongue-and-groove maple, finished in eggshell-white enamel. An all-wood court costs a minimum of $10,000, and may cost several times that amount depending on the external structure. However, the side and rear walls of some courts, and occasionally even the front wall, may be built of cement with a plaster surface. This brings the initial cost down considerably, although such courts require more yearly maintenance, since the plaster has a way of chipping off under the constant hammering of the ball.

In warm weather, masonry walls tend to sweat and thus impart some vicious skids to the ball, and at other times they have a kind of lifelessness — less real than imagined, perhaps, but depressing all the same. Certainly wood, like grass for a tennis court, is the most desirable material, but as wood and the craftsmanship required to install it become more and more expensive, the all-wood squash court will become rarer and rarer. This sad fact has its bright side, however. The cheaper the relative cost of building a court, the easier it will be for squash to gain real popularity throughout the country. And there is no doubt that cement is cheaper than wood.

Squash originated in a London prison in the early nineteenth century; it is a perfect game for shut-ins, which is what an ever-increasing number of us are becoming, as the urbanization of America continues apace. At present, nearly all the country's squash courts are contained in private men's clubs, in college and university gymnasiums, and in YMCAs. Provided that court costs can be kept low, which means cement or some yet-to-be-devised synthetic substitute for wood, there is no reason why each new apartment house or office building should not include a few courts. In sports-conscious Australia, where the lighter ball permits less sturdily built and far cheaper courts, nearly every community has its bank of public squash courts — some free, like handball courts in our city playgrounds, some available at a fee. To mention bowling and squash in the same sentence at first seems ludicrous, but there is a social and competitive side to both games that permits comparison. Although neither sportsman would want to admit it, one may overhear much the same banter, if not the same accents, beside the roaring fire in the oak-paneled locker room of New York's elite Racquet and Tennis Club and around the local lanes in Hohokus, N.J., on a league night. But there the analogy stops. Bowling is slow, deliberate, requiring enormous precision in the execution of a single basic movement. Squash is lightning-fast, requires constant improvisation, and is physically exhausting — it is by far the most tiring of all the racquet sports. When played seriously, it requires a combination of speed, endurance, and quickness of eye perhaps unmatched by any other sport save boxing. When played purely for fun it elicits these qualities from even the most lazy player. And it is quick. For harried executives seeking to exorcise the demon of overindulgence or simply to maintain their waistlines, a five-game squash match, which can be shoehorned into a lunch hour or in the time between the end of work and the 6:47 to Greenwich, is a perfect solution.

The fact that squash packs a maximum amount of exercise into every minute of play (the normal unit of time for booking a court is half an hour) is one reason why in the past five years the number of squash courts in the country has increased by 50 percent and now totals well over 2,000. There are many courts in Canada, where the long winters make the sport particularly popular, and also some courts in Mexico, where a small nucleus of avid players are beginning to boom the game.

The trend is obvious. Already in the squash facilities with which I am most familiar, the clubs in the New York metropolitan area, one must often reserve a court as long as a week in advance. On an average winter night at the University Club not one of the seven courts is idle from 5:00 to 7:30 p.m., and John Greco, the professional there, estimates that from 1968 to 1971 the number of active players more than doubled. This is only an indication of things to come. Squash, once strictly an upper-class exercise, has been introduced through the colleges and universities to thousands upon thousands of young men, nearly all of them destined to be locked into urban lives. They will, and already are, demanding an outlet for their pent-up energies. Handball provides the same quality of exercise as squash, but not the subtlety, variety and speed, and since the two require essentially the same space, squash seems to be the better choice. Very soon, control of the game may be expected to pass from the hands of the clubmen into the public domain, like tennis — this is already the case in Australia. When it does, one can expect that the level of play will improve in direct proportion to the numbers who play the game — and certainly one can expect many more courts for them to play in.

photo: Bob Lehman

COMPETITION

● I have described squash racquets as I first saw it — played by duffers. I can think of no better way, now, to give the full flavor of the game and its fine points than to describe in detail the most thrilling match I ever watched — played by champions.

The scene is the Ringe Courts at the University of Pennsylvania, where the U.S. Men's Amateur championships are being held on Washington's Birthday weekend, 1970. At approximately 11:00 a.m. on Sunday morning, one can sense an electrical charge building in the knowledgeable crowd that has filled the gallery and is pressing two-deep at the rail that runs around the upper periphery of Court No. 1, where a quarter-final-round match is in progress. All at once, the spectators draw breath. Exhaled, the communal gasp becomes two hundred individual sighs of appreciation, instantly drowned in a crashing wave of applause.

This burst of sound is occasioned by the sight of Charles Ufford, a baldish, 38-year-old lawyer from New York City, hurling his 6-foot-5½-inch, 215-pound frame forward and to his left, cocking his right wrist while in full stride, and swiping the ball viciously with his racquet. Just a split-second before, the ball had left the racquet of Ufford's opponent, Colin Adair, a wiry, 27-year-old stockbroker from Montreal, at well over 100 miles an hour and had abruptly changed its direction of flight four times: once angling off the right wall of the court, again rebounding from the front wall, a third time bouncing off the floor, and finally glancing off the left wall. There Ufford has met it and drilled it into a corner of the white-walled room so that it hit the side wall, traveled a foot, and caromed against the front wall a millimeter above the "tin" or telltale. Spinning off the front wall, the ball bounced no more than two inches off the floor, then bounced again before Adair, streaking past Ufford with all the strength of his well-conditioned body, was able to reach it.

Seated in the center of the first row of the gallery that rises steeply toward the neon-lit ceiling, his feet just above the level of the players' heads, is the referee, William T. Ketcham, Jr., an IBM executive and former president of the United States Squash Racquets Association. He leans over the iron rail and intones the score: "Point to Mr. Ufford. Mr. Ufford wins the second game, 15-14. The games are 1-all. Gentlemen, you have two minutes."

Ufford's game-winning shot, recognized by the gallery as a backhand reverse-corner, exemplifies squash racquets at its best. To begin with, it came at a time when both players had been slamming away at each other for twenty minutes and were battling not only each other but the rising tide of fatigue as well. Already Ufford's cheeks are flushed a deep crimson — later in the match they will go white. The blond Adair, called "the Bull" by his Canadian peers because of his superb conditioning, is only slightly flushed, but he is gulping great lungfuls of air after every point, and his face is gleaming with perspiration.

Physical conditioning, however, is only half the preparation needed for this sort of intense competition. Of equal importance is psychological conditioning, for although the Ufford-Adair match is only one of many held over a period of three days at the tournament, and not the championship match either (that honor was finally won, as expected, by the defending champion, Anil Nayar of Bombay, India, and Cambridge, Mass.), it is by far and away the most mentally exhausting — and most exciting, if my own reaction as well as that of the others watching with me can be taken as a measure.

Ufford's game-point shot, for instance, was all the more remarkable in that the only real choice he had to remain in contention turned on its precision. Had the ball he hit reached the front wall a few inches higher, it would have bounced higher. Adair, a former U.S. and Canadian champion, would in all likelihood have reached it and, being up front, dropped it or slashed it back past Ufford for a winner. Had it been a millimeter lower, it would have hit the telltale with a resounding clang and been called "down." In either case, Adair would have won the point and the game, taking an all but insurmountable lead in the match. The knowledge must have perched like a specter somewhere on the edge of Ufford's consciousness when he made the stroke. Ignoring it — or facing it — he had shown the cool of a golf pro lining up a 10-foot putt worth $10,000.

There *are* weekend tournaments in which several thousand dollars may change hands — based on the outcome of the matches and the arcane dictates of an institution called a Calcutta pool — yet money plays no part in the stakes at the Nationals. Pride is everything. For Adair it is personal and national pride. When he had won the U.S. title in 1968 in Boston in an all-Canadian final, having beaten the top American, Samuel P. Howe III, in the semifinals, the taste of victory had been soured by the knowledge that Howe, along with other Americans, had been ailing with intestinal flu.

Indeed, defending his title the next year, Adair had fallen in the quarter-finals to an American player who was not even seeded. Then, in 1970, just the previous weekend in Montreal, Howe had eliminated Adair from the Canadian championships, which cost him his Canadian title. Now, if Adair beats Ufford, as he is expected to do and as he had easily done in Boston in 1968, he will get another crack at Howe, in the semifinals to be played that afternoon, and a chance to regain some of his lost luster. The Bull is very proud and very hungry.

For Ufford, at thirty-eight, with only one more season to play before he turns forty and becomes a Veteran, eligible to compete in that separate class for the aged and infirm, this tournament has become a swan song. Adair is favored to win; but Ufford, who in his day has won practically every honor in squash *except* the Nationals, is a supreme stylist with an extraordinary "touch" for so big a man, and he has the game to beat Adair if only he can put it all together. And if he does not tire. That is the key; for not only is Ufford giving eleven years to his younger opponent, whose game is based primarily on his marvelous ability to run all day and hit like a bull, but the day before Ufford has played two grueling matches against much younger players.

Mr. Ufford   photo: Bob Lehman

In the first, on Saturday morning, he barely squeaked by Eliot Berry, Penn's soccer-style place kicker and the No. 2 player on Penn's varsity squash team. Berry, his shoulder-length hair held out of his eyes by a Navajo headband, with nothing to lose and everything to gain from beating his more experienced opponent, pulled out all the stops and played the match of his life. At the end of the first game, which Berry won, 17-14, Ufford snapped his $30 racquet over his knee in seeming disgust. Actually, the racquet had cracked during the match and Ufford was simply administering the *coup de grace*. After that, Ufford lost the second game as well and had only managed to salvage the match by extending himself to the fullest, laying open the fourth finger of his racquet hand against the floor in the process and smearing his white shorts with blood.

The match with Berry had been one that he had expected to win without trouble. But his next match was another story. It was with Larry Terrell, the intercollegiate champion, who plays No. 1 on the Harvard University team, the perennial collegiate powerhouse in the game (Ufford played No. 1 for Harvard in 1952 and 1953). Terrell was not only seventeen years younger than Ufford and in top shape but also a superb stylist who hadn't lost a match all season in college play. Having seen the draw before coming to Philadelphia, and knowing that once he got by Berry he would certainly meet Terrell in the second round, Ufford had brought only one set of shorts. Consequently, he had appeared against Terrell on Saturday afternoon wearing the same blood-stained togs that he had worn that morning; and, incredibly, he had won.

Now on Sunday, in the same court, Ufford's shorts, though a pristine white, are tight around his 38-inch waist. They belong to his father, a professor of physics at Penn who, in the company of his own and his son's wife, is watching from the top of the gallery and wondering if, incredibly, Ufford may not win again. The court they are playing on is one of two in the Ringe complex, in the shadow of the University's Franklin Field, arranged in such a way that spectators can peer down into it from all sides, rather than simply from the rear gallery, as is more common. Those, plus sixteen other courts, one with a glass rear wall, make the Ringe complex probably the finest squash facility in the world.

Having taken the permissible two-minute break between the second and third games to rest and towel themselves off, Ufford and Adair have entered the court again through the small door in the rear wall and are preparing to resume play.

Mr. Adair
photo: Bob Lehman

In the American game of squash — as opposed to badminton, say, or the English version of squash, in which only the server can score — every winning ball counts a point for the player who makes it. The player making a point serves the next one, and a game is won by the player who reaches 15 first (the English play to nine). However, if the score has been tied at 13-13, the player who held the lead before the tie has an option of playing to 15, 16, or 18 points; and if the tie comes at 14-14, he may choose to play to 15 or 17. All of which only illustrates what those who are seeking to restructure the scoring of tennis well know: that racquet sports, like English spelling, retain certain idiosyncracies based more on tradition than on logic. A game in squash is the rough equivalent of a set in tennis, and as in tennis, a match is three out of five.

Ufford and Adair, therefore, tied at one game apiece, will have to play at least two more games, possibly three, to see which of them will advance to the semifinals, scheduled for 5:00 that afternoon.

In all, thirty-five of the best amateurs in the world commenced play in this tournament on Saturday, with three preliminary matches held Friday night. The losers have been dropping by the wayside. For Nayar, the eventual winner, and for the runner-up, the American Sam Howe, it will mean a lot of squash — two matches on Saturday and two on Sunday, with the final and deciding match late Monday morning.

But to the spectators who hang around the eighteen courts in the Ringe complex for the full three days of play, it means total saturation, since, concurrent with the major event, three other tournaments are being held. These are the National Veterans (for men forty years or over, with a field of forty-eight players — won for the fourth time in a row by Boston's legendary Henri Salaun), the National Seniors (men fifty years or over, twenty-four players — won by Calvin MacCracken, just turned fifty), and the National Team. This third

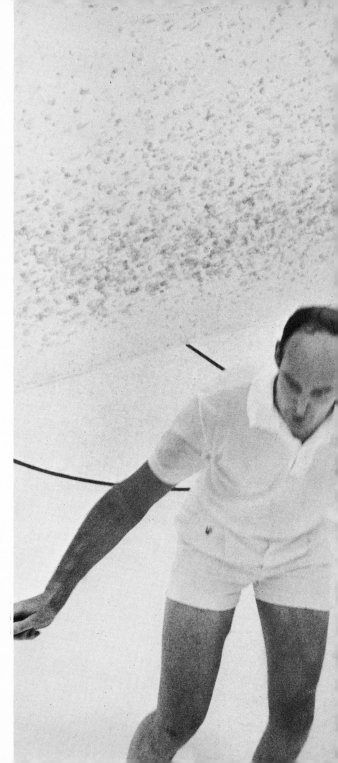

photo: Bob Lehman

photo: Bob Lehman

tournament consists of twenty-five teams of five players each, representing cities and regions as far apart as Mexico City and Ontario, Boston and British Columbia, together with colleges, universities, service academies, and even one family — three brothers named Foster and two of their teenage sons, eliminated in the first round. Because of its size, the New York metropolitan area has sent two teams, which is the reason that I am present that weekend, playing in the last position on the second New York team. We were not eliminated in the first round like the Fosters, but we did bow in the second to a strong Philadelphia team, while the No. 1 New York team made it to the finals before losing to Ontario, the defending champions.

31

These three tournaments bring together a total of 276 players who will compete in 242 matches in all before the winners are sifted out. Add to the players a proportionate number of wives, sweethearts, college coaches, USSRA officials, sponsors and patrons of the game, supply them with lapel tags and a full social program of meetings, lunches, cocktails, and a dinner dance at Penn's Gimbel Gymnasium on Saturday night, and, despite the preponderance of button-down collars and club ties, you have a typical American convention. It would be difficult to distinguish, say, from the convention of the Antique Automobile Club of America — which, as it happens, is also headquartered this weekend at the Bellevue Stratford in Philadelphia. When someone in a Bellevue elevator says he is about to do a little body restoration it is a toss-up whether he intends to polish a fender or loll in a steam bath before his next match.

At the Ringe Courts, Ufford is standing with his right foot in a quarter circle drawn in the forward outside corner of the right serving box. As in tennis, special rules govern the serve. A red line drawn across the floor of the court 10 feet out from the back wall delineates the serving area, which is divided down the middle into a right and left box. The point at which the dividing line and the transverse line meet at right angles is called the T and is the strategic position to hold. A good player standing on the T can get to almost any shot his opponent can make.

Since he won the previous game, Ufford serves the first ball of the third game — a lob. It strikes high up on the front wall, well above the 6½-foot service line, which it must clear to be good. Only the serve, in squash, is required to touch the front wall before hitting any other. Leaving the front wall, the ball continues in a high arc, just missing the ceiling, looping back, and kissing the left wall deep on Adair's side of the court, where it drops into the box opposite the one Ufford served from. There, Adair must play it so close to the wall that all he can do is return it, without any chance of making an attacking shot.

Cutting it so fine that he nicks the wall with his racquet, Adair pastes a rail shot straight down the wall and back again, trying in his turn to keep the ball as close as possible. Ufford, moving from the T, angles back and to his left to play the ball, while Adair, darting out of the way even before finishing his stroke, takes his position on the T. Eventually, after a lightning exchange of short shots up front, Adair, quicker on his feet than Ufford, wins the point.

Adair serves and loses the next point, and eventually he loses the game at 15-8, as Ufford, in top form, mixing gently caressed shots that drop dead off the front wall with drives that keep Adair deep in the court, forces error after error. Once more Ketcham intones the score, this time reminding the players that they have five minutes' rest.

Those on the edge of the crowd drift off to peer into adjacent courts, where the thwack of balls on wood and an occasional cry of anguish give evidence of dramas still in progress. And moving out in concentric circles through space and time from the Ringe Courts, one can imagine the same play repeated thousands of times each week from November to April in clubs, armories, gymnasiums, and Y's around the country, without crowds to cheer or referees to judge, with just two men together in a white-walled room, courteously pounding the ball as if their mortal souls depended on it.

In the New York metropolitan area alone, there are more than five hundred registered squash players belonging to forty member clubs. These play a full schedule of matches against each other in four separate leagues (not all of the clubs field teams in each of the leagues).

Besides the team matches, there are invitation tournaments on nearly every weekend of the season, usually with attendant social activities, particularly in the suburban clubs. There are also tournaments to decide the champions within each league.

All this feverish and not inexpensive activity (yearly dues to metropolitan clubs range from $300 to $500, and there is also a court fee — usually $1 — and equipment cost, possibly as high as $100 a season for someone who is hard on racquets and shoes) traces its origin to a debtors' prison in London, sometime around 1800. With time on their hands and walls on each side, the inmates of Fleet Prison evolved the game of hard racquets, or simply racquets. This game, played in a slate-walled gallery the size of a tennis court, with a ball tightly wound like a miniature baseball but having the bounce of a five-and-dime Superball, eventually found its way into the English public schools.

At one of these — Harrow — the only racquets court was in such constant demand that those waiting to play sought some way of warming up outside before their brief turn came. Their answer was a soft, India-rubber ball that could be swatted against a wall with all the pace of the hard racquets ball but would not then bound off across the moors. (A good equivalent is the present-day whiffle ball that suburban golfers can drive on their front lawns.) Harrow's rubber ball, unlike the present-day American ball, was so soft that its sides could be pressed together between thumb and forefinger. In short, it squashed; and so the game of squash rackets (as the British spell it) was born at Harrow in the 1880's.

From there it spread to Oxford and Cambridge and around the world with the British raj. What better way for an English officer and gentleman to keep fit in such bloody awful parts of the world as India, Pakistan, and Egypt — three countries whose nationals, along with the Australians, now dominate the sport. Squash entered the United States from Canada toward the end of the nineteenth century. Here it developed a hybrid, or American, form in the hothouse atmosphere of the Ivy League colleges and private clubs of Boston, New York, and Philadelphia, and it became a sport in a class with polo and yachting.

There was a time when gentlemanly conduct included the exclusion of Jews and Negroes from most of the private men's clubs in the land. Today such prejudice seems less gentlemanly. But the fact remains that, within the thick stone walls and arrogant architecture of the likes of New York City's University Club and the Racquet and Tennis Club, prejudice has a way of hanging on like malaria. In the memory of the elder statesmen of squash, only one black face has been seen on the squash circuit, and that player seems already to have dropped from view.

In the New York metropolitan area, Jewish players belong either to one of the citys' Ivy League clubs, where the barriers have been down for some decades, or to one of several strictly Jewish clubs. There is no lack of cordiality between Jewish and Wasp clubs, but there have been no mergers either. In fact, the only serious disturbance to upset the equanimity of the squash world grew out of just this situation. By some quirk that still has jowls wagging in the deep leather chairs in clubs from Boston to Philadelphia, the finest squash talent to appear on the scene during the mid-sixties came not from the vaunted Merion Cricket Club of Philadelphia, or out of the Eastern prep schools, but from Brighton Beach, Brooklyn.

His name was Victor Niederhoffer and he was a Jew. After seeing squash for the first time as a freshman at Harvard, in 1960, Niederhoffer, a strong tennis player, switched racquets and in short order won every squash tournament in sight, and in 1966 he took the Nationals. But the next year, as a graduate student at the University of Chicago, he refused to defend his title, claiming that the Chicago clubs, hosts that year to the Nationals, had refused him membership because of prejudice. The clubs vehemently denied this. They just did not like him, they said.

In 1968, after two years of playing practically no competitive squash, Niederhoffer teamed with Victor Elmaleh (also Jewish and also a fine player, although at 49 well past his prime) and won the National doubles title. With that extraordinary accomplishment behind him, there was very little left for Niederhoffer to prove, and he all but abandoned the game. He was above all else a fierce and dedicated competitor, and his loss of interest in squash must be attributed in part to his understanding that the prejudice he had been fighting was also a battle won — against, as it turned out, a not overly tenacious foe. The old guard, with right on its side, will fight on. When wrong, it has a way of giving up with disarming grace.

Ufford and Adair resume their match. As they begin the fourth game, Adair, who knows he must win this game to remain in the tournament, appears to take charge. Ufford, however, his cheeks now white with exhaustion, is still making enough brilliant shots to keep Adair from running away with the game. But his long legs are not carrying him around the court with the same speed as in the beginning of the match. Time and again he is late getting to one of Adair's drives.

Then, with Adair leading, 9-8, Ufford plays a point that declares unmistakably to the crowd and to Adair that he is going for broke. Appearing to be hopelessly out of reach of a ball, he makes a desperation dive, hitting it just as he sprawls full length on the floor. Adair, caught off guard, makes a weak return, which Ufford bats back while still down in the center of the court. Adair cannot get around him and cannot reach the ball; so he calls a "let." The point will be played over.

In tennis one plays a let when a serve ticks the net, or when a dog runs onto the court and bites the ball. In squash, however, one plays a let whenever one player unnecessarily impedes the other from getting to or hitting the ball. It happens a lot in that crowded little room, and it is as integral a part of the game as the foul rule in basketball. It happens also to be both the flaw and the glory of squash racquets — the flaw because the word "unnecessary" is so impossible to interpret, the glory because it puts a premium on the sort of sportsmanship and gentlemanly behavior that so endears the game to those East Coast Brahmins who have nursed it so assiduously for so long. When all is said and done, only the player himself can really judge whether he could have moved out of the way, while only the man calling for the let knows for sure whether he could have reached the ball if he had been alone in the court. If the game is being played with a referee, a player *asks* for a let, but playing without a referee, the decision as to whether he has been hindered is his.

In this case there is no doubt. Ufford was entitled to dive for the ball and then to hit from his knees as long as he was able. Nor was there any doubt that, having done so, he was in no position to leap nimbly out of Adair's way, while Adair plainly could not reach the ball over Ufford's prostrate body.

When the point is replayed, Adair wins it. But Ufford fights back and ties the score at 13-13; and Adair, whose choice it is, elects to play a "set of 5," that is, to 18 points, feeling that time and the ravages of exhaustion are on his side. The score mounts, and Ufford gains the edge. He is on the brink now, leading 17-16 — one point and he will win the match. He has his chance when Adair, driven deep, can only manage a weak return that plops off the front wall like a sitting duck. Ufford is on top of it with plenty of time — perhaps too much time, for he seems to hesitate, undecided whether he should drop it or slam it deep. Instead of doing either, he drives it into the tin, one of the few outright errors he has made all day. Seventeen all.

Ufford walks back to receive Adair's serve, shaking his head and rolling his eyes toward the gallery. Perhaps he is remembering the fifth game of a match he played against David Watts in that very same court when, in 1961, the Nationals was last held in Philadelphia. Like this one, it was a quarter-final match, but that time Ufford, at the peak of his game, was seeded No. 1 in the tournament and had brought clothes for the full three days. In the fifth game with Watts, he led 14-6, which meant that to lose the match he would have to lose at least nine straight points — and he did. "You know, Charlie," a friend said, "that court owes you something." Was this, he may now be wondering, the way he is to be repaid?

Adair serves — not a conventional lob serve, which is safe and conserves energy, but a hard, smashing overhead that breaks off the side wall and angles down toward Ufford's feet. Adair is hoping that with Ufford's reactions slowed by fatigue, he may botch his return. But Ufford does as much as he can with it, blocking it back down the left wall. They exchange shots, and then with Ufford just a fraction slow to move out of the way, Adair asks for a let. Earlier in the game he would have unhesitatingly charged past Ufford to hit the ball, but now he will not take that chance; moreover, it gives him another opportunity to face Ufford with his fast serve.

Adair serves; they exchange shots, and this time Ufford stops play by asking for a let. Then, instead of serving again, Adair tosses the ball up to the referee, who squeezes it between thumb and forefinger. The thick rubber shell is cracked along the seam. Picking a new ball out of his blazer pocket, Ketcham tosses it down to the players.

There is a audible release of tension in the crowd, while Ufford and Adair bang the new ball up against the front wall thirty or forty times to warm it up. It is not unusual for squash balls to break during a hard-fought match, and since its bounce (less than half that of a tennis ball) depends on the temperature of the air inside it, the ball must be warmed up. The broken ball may be just the break Ufford needs at this critical point in the match, giving him two valuable minutes to catch his breath and gather his remaining strength.

photo: B. Swett

When both players are satisfied with the bounce, Adair serves a third time at 17-17. Ufford blocks back the shot; they rally, and Adair calls let. Three more times the sequence is repeated, with variations. Once Adair's serve is too hot for Ufford to handle. He misses it completely, but then, spinning wildly, he manages to hit it on his second try as it leaps high off the back wall. And Adair calls let. So far this final point has been played six times.

Now Adair serves a seventh time, and black lightning strikes at Ufford's feet. He backhands the shot down the left wall. Adair slugs a backhand with all his might cross-court, drawing Ufford off the T to his right. He hits a rail shot along the forehand wall — high and safe. Adair lets it go to the back wall, where he takes it on the rebound and slams a cross-court to Ufford's backhand, hoping that it will catch the crack between the sidewall and the floor for a "nick" and roll dead.

Instead, it angles out far enough for Ufford to try a forehand shot into the left corner. It is a good one, but Adair reaches it, with no time, however, to do more than swat it back along the backhand wall. Ufford now hits a perfectly angled cross-court that bounces and breaks deep off the right-hand wall. Adair, who is already moving back to the T, continues back and to his right. He reaches the ball, but he is off balance.

He tries for a deep cross-court drive, but the stroke is weak, and the angle is wrong. The ball hits the front wall and then, instead of carrying straight back, breaks off the side wall and toward Ufford, who is set on the T. Ufford steps forward, catching the ball on a half volley, just as it comes off the floor, and with the same flick of his wrist that won him the second game, strokes the ball into the corner to his right — side wall, front wall, floor.

Adair is moving at top speed along the diagonal of the court — from back right to front left, the court's longest dimension. He reaches out; he dives, hitting the ball, but at the very instant that he connects, he calls out, "Not up."

Better than any one of the two hundred spectators, the referee or the two judges, he knows that the ball has bounced twice, and rather than leave what would be an excruciating call for the referee, he calls himself out — and out of the tournament. The applause for both men, as they embrace in midcourt, is deafening and long.

Those in the gallery have seen what they came for. They have seen speed, and grace, and exhaustion overcome. And more than anything, they have seen gentlemen at play.

In the lobby afterward, buttoning their camel's-hair coats over their lapel tags, lighting their briars, chatting in cultured, excited tones about the match, the spectators prepare to leave for lunch. Pushing through them, like a fish swimming against the tide, is a long-haired, scruffy-bearded Penn student in levis and tattered sweater. He pays little attention to the crowd as he makes his deliberate way to a bulletin board posted on a far wall headed "Ringe Squash Court Daily Reservations." Written across the Saturday and Sunday and the morning hours of Monday in big blue pencil is the single peremptive word NATIONALS. Already two-thirds of the Monday-afternoon courts are booked, and the student has to study the chart a moment before he can find a spot to add his name. Squash is on its way.

BASICS

THE SINGLES GAME

● In the broad field of athletics, squash belongs to the racquets clan — more particularly to that family of racquet sports played against a wall. Squash opponents, without a net to keep things tidy, must share the same confined space, while simultaneously practicing the basic principle of racquet sports: alternating turns. And just *there* lies the special schizophrenia of squash: to do your damnedest to keep your opponent from hitting the ball at one instant, and in the very next instant to take equal pains not to abridge his right to do so. This rapid-fire change of polarity, like alternating current, is a hard concept to grasp in theory. Yet in practice it works.

Reduced to its bare bones, the challenge of squash is this: by striking the ball with your racquet, cause it to hit the front wall of the court and then bounce twice on the floor. That, essentially, is all there is to it. Accomplish that feat and you win a point. Do it often enough and you win the game and the match.

Even in an old folks' home or a nursery school you would have to pick carefully to come up with someone who couldn't produce the desired effect with the ball if left to his own devices. But, of course, in squash, as in most sports, you are not left to your own devices. There is an opposing force in the court with you intent on not letting your ball bounce twice on the floor, while trying in his turn to make it happen when he hits the ball. Whereupon you step in and frustrate his attempt. And so it goes, until one of you misses.

Thus, every time you hit the ball the move embodies both offensive and defensive elements — offensive, in that if you hit the ball so that it reaches the front wall, it becomes a potential point; defensive, in that by hitting the ball before its second bounce, you are nullifying your opponent's try for a point. Depending on the strategic situation, some shots weigh heavily on the offensive side, some on the defensive; but always both elements are present.

This distinction is certain to become blurred the moment you pick up a racquet and begin to worry about such incidental problems as how and where to hit the ball most effectively, yet it is the common root from which all moves in squash, no matter how complicated, ultimately stem.

There is one other concept basic to squash that should be fixed firmly at the outset: your obligation, after hitting the ball, to give your opponent full opportunity within his capacity of mind and muscle to hit it before it bounces twice on the floor — or, if he so chooses, before it bounces even once. (He cannot, however, within the rules, intereferε with it before it has hit the front wall.)

Your obligation to give him free access is, in a word, absolute. The moment the ball leaves your racquet, you should, ideally, vanish from the court. This being impossible, you must see to it that you occupy only a part of the court that your opponent demonstrably has no use for in his pursuit of the ball. This means two things. First, depending on your relative positions, there will be certain parts of the court into which you cannot hit the ball, since no matter how agile you are it would be impossible for you to get out of the way afterward. And second, having hit the ball, your prime consideration cannot be moving into a favorable position to field the next shot, but must be to get out of the way. Failing either of these, your opponent *may* stop play by calling a let. I stress *may*, because he may on the other hand choose to continue play, if he sees an advantage in it, and thus you are giving him a choice, which either way is a big plus for him.

Beyond these underlying principles of squash racquets, everything else is detail and training, the endless refinements that make one player better than another.

CONDITIONING

● A few topflight players get in shape to play squash. Most others play squash to get in shape. The game demands it. No matter how good or bad you are, as long as you are playing with someone approximately your speed — preferably just a bit better — you find that the ball has a tantalizing way of beckoning to you, and no matter how tired you are, you can always summon up the strength for one more lunge to scrape it out of the back corner.

Squash has this reputation, and I wish I had the court fee for every paunchy young executive who after his second martini says, "No more of these lunches, Harry. Let's you and I try squash next week." And if next week ever comes, it may find them booked into a court at the Yale Club passing a sweaty half-hour, huffing and puffing. But unless they reserve the court again for later the same week, and keep to that schedule in the weeks that follow, that is all their squash will be, sweating and huffing and puffing.

Squash is not like skiing or golf or tennis, which can be played moderately well from time to time, with long layoffs in between. You do need wind and you do need to have legs capable of sudden starts and stops. Fortunately for those who hate exercise, playing the game, providing you do it regularly, is as much conditioning as you need.

One precaution, however. It is a good idea, particularly in the beginning of a season, or when you are tired, to stretch and loosen your muscles before going into the court. There is probably no sport more likely to give the out-of-condition player a torn Achilles tendon or ripped calf muscle than squash.

A popped muscle in the calf feels at first gasp just as though your opponent had hit you lightly with his racquet — but the subsequent pain can be intense. More than once I have seen a player whirl and glare in bewilderment at his opponent who happens to be on the other side of the court, and then crumple on the floor clutching his leg.

I've even done it twice myself. Fortunately, in both cases it was only a torn calf muscle, which ordinarily will heal by itself within one to four weeks. Ordinarily, a torn muscle does not require special attention, although there is always the possibility of complications caused by internal bleeding. Should the swelling and pain persist, therefore, one should consult a doctor. Meanwhile, walking will be greatly eased if the heel is raised slightly, either by taping several layers of cardboard inside the shoe or by inserting a heel pad that can be bought in any drugstore.

If the Achilles tendon goes, that is something else again, requiring immediate medical care and a costly, although routine, operation that may keep you sidelined for as long as a year. Once healed, however, the tendon should be good as new, as several players I know will attest. To prevent either eventuality, deep kneebends and any other motions that stretch and warm up the calf muscles before you start are the best precautions.

photo: B. Swett

If you are going to be playing your squash at a club where there is a professional who sells racquets and clothing, buy them from him. You may be paying up to 20 percent more than at a cut-rate sporting goods store, but the extra money will be well spent in terms of services and good will. It is the pro, after all, who will be looking after your things, mending the frayed strings in your racquet, and taking the bookings for a court, for which, if your club is typical, there will be a demand that far outreaches the supply. If you do buy from him, take his advice.

EQUIPMENT

If you are going to have to outfit yourself, any clothes will do as long as they are comfortable, washable, and white. The first two qualities are as obvious as they are optional. The third, however — wearing whites — is specified in the rules. With everything happening so fast in squash, bits of color on a player's person can only add to the visual confusion. Frequently, this rule is overlooked. Many of the younger, long-haired players today go in for gaudy headbands to keep their combined tresses and sweat out of their eyes.

Tennis sweaters, shirts, and shorts are appropriate. Long trousers are still worn on occasion. They are good for playing in cold courts if you are slow to warm up. They also serve to protect your legs from the inevitable nicks one gets from the racquet — one's own, more often than not.

As for sneakers, comfort is the prime criterion. If the courts you are playing on have been painted properly — that is, if the right amount of pumice has been added to the paint on the floor — slipping should be no problem. If, however, the floors are slippery, sneakers with a deck-gripping tread are preferable to those with a smooth rubber sole. Increasingly, one sees leather sneakers on the squash courts. They offer excellent support and cushioning, and, surprisingly, they are lighter than most canvas shoes. Their only drawback, in fact, is their cost — two to three times that of ordinary sneakers. But for people who are not hard on their sneakers (those who do not drag their toes or make a lot of quick, jerky steps) they should last two to three times as long, and so cost no more in the long run.

There are three major manufacturers of American-weight racquets: Cragin, Bancroft, and Wilson. Each makes a variety of models and sells them at a variety of prices, starting as low as $10 and reaching above $30. The chances are that if you are beginning the game, a modestly priced racquet is what you want. It will last almost as long as an expensive racquet, and the difference in performance will hardly be perceptible. Do, however, make sure that the racquet feels comfortable, that the balance is right for you and that the grip fits your hand.

The better racquets are sold unstrung. The cost of stringing will be from $8 to $15, depending on the material. Sheep gut is preferred because of its elasticity. However, it costs more and wears out faster than good nylon — and again, the beginner won't be able to tell the difference. In fact, despite what they say, I doubt whether many experts can.

Nothing frays gut faster than dampness — putting it in a bag with sweaty clothes, for instance. You do not need a press, but a rubberized waterproof cover is a good idea.

With balls you have quite a choice. And here there is quite a difference. There are two makes of American squash ball; Cragin and Seamless. The Cragin has a green diamond inlaid in its surface (two green diamonds in the livelier doubles ball). The Seamless is all black, and like the Cragin ball, has a seam. Both balls perform within the limits set by the USSRA — that is, they are made of black inflated rubber, are 1.75 inches in diameter, and if dropped from a height of 100 inches onto a solid base in a room temperature of 65°F, they will rebound 24 to 26 inches. In play, however, the Cragin ball seems harder and plays faster, whereas the Seamless as it heats up during play becomes soft and bounces higher and slower off the floor. But that is the situation as of this writing. Next year the companies may change their formulas, as they have in the past, and the situation could be reversed.

Cragin also makes a summer ball, meant to perform like a regular ball but in temperatures of 80 and 90 degrees. The summer ball makes the game much more enjoyable in hot weather, when it used to be all but impossible to make a winning shot with temperatures causing the ball to bound about the court like a jackrabbit. Generally you will find players favoring one ball over the other — recently the Cragin has been on top — but in order to keep the grand American spirit of competition operating the USSRA will specify that the Cragin ball be used in certain tournaments, the Seamless in others.

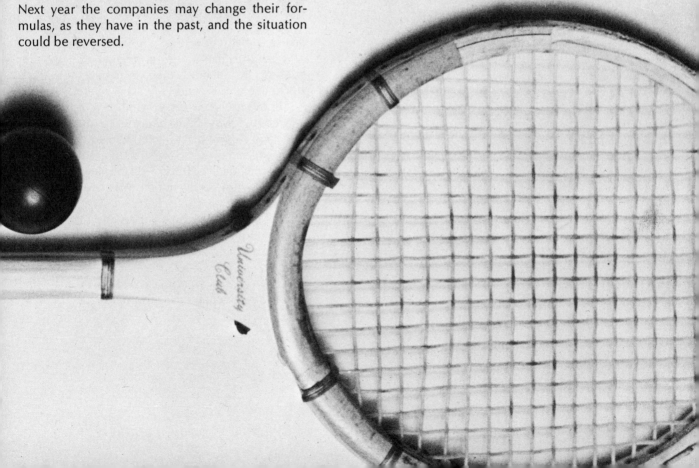

GRIP

The usual piece of capsule advice on gripping a squash racquet is to hold it as you would a hammer. The analogy is apt, not only because it positions the racquet properly in your fist, but also because it emphasizes the idea that the racquet is a tool for doing a job. Think of it as an extension of your arm that adds two feet to your reach and enables you to hit the ball with far greater force and spin than you could with your bare hand.

For both the forehand and backhand stroke, this is done with a flailing action, which has the effect of concentrating and multiplying the force of a stroke at the point and instant of impact. Your forearm and racquet, hinged at the wrist, resemble the sort of hand flails once used to thresh wheat. Its effectiveness depends largely on the flexibility of the wrist, but you will find, after a bit of experimentation, that your wrist bends freely only in one plane. The underlying principle for gripping the racquet, then, is to take maximum advantage of this bend.

An example is in order. Anil Nayar, superbly tutored by two of the game's top mentors, the Pakistani Yusuf Khan (no relation to the Hashim Khan squash dynasty) and Jack Barnaby of Harvard, conceded to be the top college coach, is making a slow, error-ridden start on his way to winning his second U.S. championship.

After each mistake he pantomimes the shot in slow motion several times as it should have been played, but he does this with the flat of his hand in place of the racquet. The point is that the motion his arm and wrist make should be the same with the empty hand as with the racquet.

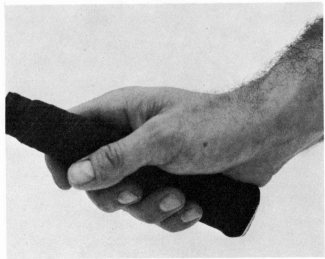

Rather than using the whole hand to simulate the racquet face, use instead the tip of your forefinger. Go through these motions and mental contortions, and you should arrive at a proper and effective grip. Extend your arm out full length, with your palm perpendicular to the floor. Now point with your forefinger and by a leap of imagination conceive of your forefinger as being a squash racquet, your fleshy fingerprint the forehand face of the racquet, the nail the backhand. Swing your arm back and forth, snapping your hand at the wrist so that the fingerprint hits an imaginary ball at the moment it is moving fastest. That is the basic stroke, the forehand going one way, the backhand the other.

Now, keeping the forefinger extended along the handle, slip the racquet into your fist, gripping it with your thumb and three remaining fingers. The racquet face should lie in the same plane as your fingernail. Swing the racquet back and forth until you feel your forefinger growing like Pinocchio's nose and becoming part and parcel of the racquet. Once you have established that feeling in your mind, you can allow your forefinger to curl slightly around the racquet, to give you a stronger grip, as shown in the picture at the left.

This will feel awkward at first, but eventually you will grow used to it, and always you will have a feeling of exactly where your racquet is going and should go through the agency of your forefinger.

This grip, sometimes called the Continental Grip, is the same for the forehand and the backhand. It may not allow you to put quite as much weight behind a power shot as you could if you were gripping the racquet tightly in your fist. But remember, it isn't weight that you want — the ball, after all, weighs barely more than an ounce — it is speed and precision, and for that the forefinger is the key.

SHOTS AND TACTICS

photo: B. Swett

FOREHAND

There is only one way to learn the strokes in squash. Go into the court by yourself and practice until they feel right. Hit the ball to the front wall with your forehand — and hit it and hit it and hit it again until it goes just where you want it, time and time again. Then do the same with your backhand.

Here are some principles governing the forehand drive, which may be hit up and down the wall, cross-court, or into the corners. Learn them by heart so you can free your mind for more heady thoughts when facing an opponent.

photo: B. Swett

Stance roughly parallel to the intended return:
Your body's weight starts on the right foot and
moves to the left foot as the stroke is made. The
more "body" you put into your stroke, the more
powerful the stroke will be. But the only way to put
your weight behind your shot is to be set; that is, to
have your body poised whether you are waiting
for the ball or moving toward it, or, as sometimes
happens, moving away from it to give yourself
room to swing. Because it can be done with wrist
alone, it is easy to hit a squash ball without being
set. Indeed, it is often necessary to do so — defensively. But the shot will be relatively soft. So
beware. Do not get into bad habits even though
you can get away with them with yourself or with
another beginner.

Knees bent: The telltale is only 17 inches high.
To hit the ball with full force at that level you
need to crouch. Use your knees as an elevator to
position you vertically.

Arm back: This is largely a matter of mind. Too
often one waits until he has decided on the shot
he intends before cocking his racquet arm. This
is wrong. You will rush your shot, commit yourself before you need to, and take the precision
edge off your swing by forcing your arm to reverse its direction too suddenly. It is far better to
determine only that you will be making a forehand or a backhand. Then get your racquet back,
cocking your arm the same way for a drop, drive,
cross-court, lob, or corner shot. You will have
plenty of time to decide the exact shot as you
swing forward, and you will keep your opponent
guessing until the last possible instant.

Elbow bent: This provides some of the snap, and it allows you to get the racquet back and still keep it close to you and in control.

Wrist cocked: This is the focal point of the stroke. As the world master Hashim Khan has said about the wrist in squash, "You can't slam a closed door."

Eye on the ball: This is the key to making any shot. No matter how long you play the game, a ball will never come at you in exactly the same way twice. Like the LEM descending on the moon, constantly receiving radar feedback, you must be provided with the information necessary to make the crucial last-instant adjustments to hit the ball just so. Your radar is your eye. Keep it on the ball. No rule is more important than that.

There are two reasons why people look up at the last instant. One is vanity: You imagine that your shot is going to be sensational, and you don't want to miss a bit of it, so for a split second you become a spectator, looking at the front wall to watch the ball shave the tin. If it does, and if you see it, you are lucky, not good. There is more excuse for the second reason, but the result is just as disastrous: You are uncertain of your exact position on the court, and just before hitting the ball you make a last minute check on where the target — a point on the front wall — is. You need not do this. You will discover, after only a very few hours in the court, that you know it almost as well as the back of your hand. You rarely see a squash player smack into the wall because he isn't looking. Learning the feel of the court is one of the things you get from practice. What you gain by looking up to see where your shot should go, will be paid for manyfold by your inability to put it there. So *don't look up.*

Cracking the whip: The stroke is similar to throwing a baseball sidearm. The racquet should strike the ball at a point just forward of the left knee. The follow-through for the first few inches — while the strings that have stretched with the ball are propelling it forward — should be in the direction of the ball's flight, then it should hook sharply back toward your body. Do not take the tennis roundhouse swing. For one thing, it might take your opponent's head off and cut the game short, and for another, he may be inspired to answer in kind.

Timing is everything — work on that first. Later you can add power. But power without timing is useless.

As in golf, the best swing is one that is grooved. If your motions are nearly identical every time you hit the ball you will not only have more assurance yourself, but you will be giving your opponent the least amount of information. The variations that will determine whether you hit a ball up and down the wall or cross-court, for example, should be imparted at the last instant, by timing and follow-through. The pace should come from the speed and snap of your stroke, not from the amount or lack of backswing. Another last-instant adjustment is the angle of your racquet face. By a very slight twist of your forearm you can hit the ball with a so-called open face, a backward slant of about 20 degrees. This will give the ball a backspin, causing it to slant sharply down off the front wall, bouncing sooner and giving your opponent less time to field it. Most shots are hit with this underspin.

Yusuf Khan

BACKHAND

● Step up to a wall and place your racquet hand against it, waist-high, and push with all your might. Automatically you will have placed your palm against the wall, because you can put more power into your effort that way. Now turn your hand over so that the back of the hand is against the wall and try pushing. You have just discovered the essential reason why the forehand is a more powerful stroke than the backhand. The difference lies in the way the human body is put together.

Now take a pencil and with the point push a small wadded-up scrap of paper across a desk or table top. The chances are good that you will instinctively use a miniature backhand motion, similar to brushing crumbs off your lap. The backhand does not have the power of the forehand stroke. But, as the paper wad and pencil illustrate, the backhand is more precise and can be better controlled. If a player could choose each time he hits the ball from which side to address it, he would be wise to use the backhand for placements, the forehand for drives, only varying the procedure to confuse his opponent.

Sharif Khan

Only occasionally, however, do you actually have that choice. When slamming an overhead, for instance, you use your forehand; defensively punching back a shot hit directly at you, you use a backhand. But ordinarily it is your opponent who determines which stroke you will use, by hitting the ball to your left or to your right. One exception to this is when the ball caroms off the side wall, bounces, and then rebounds off the middle of the back wall. In this case the man playing it has the option of backing to the left, say, if the ball is coming off the forehand wall, and hitting it on his forehand. Or he can "turn" on the ball, following it with his eyes and body and playing it, as he and the ball complete their turn, off his backhand. There are advantages to each way, and they will be discussed later.

The problem, then, because of the basic difference between the two strokes, is to concentrate on timing and placement when working on your forehand, and on power when working on the backhand. The ultimate refinement of the backhand is to put as much of your body into the stroke as possible.

Like all strokes in squash, the backhand works best when all the parts of the body are positioned properly and working in coordination. The feet are positioned on an axis roughly perpendicular to the front wall, the shoulders are in the same plane, the eyes on the ball, the racquet is cocked back as far as it will go. Another reason that the backhand is the beginner's best stroke is that the nature of the stroke tends to keep the player positioned properly. This is particularly true if you have to make a long reach for the ball, forcing you to lead with your right foot, extending your body low to the floor, as shown on page 62. At the same time you can use your left hand, assuming you are right-handed, to pull your racquet all the way back across your chest so that your hand is gripping it at a position near your left shoulder, and the racquet face itself is curled around behind your head. From this position the stroke comes like the uncoiling of a powerful spring, but the power comes from the speed of the stroke and the timing, not so much from the weight of the body behind it.

Racquet contact with the ball should be made slightly in front of the right foot, flicking the ball either straight down the wall, cross-court, or into one of the corners. A proper backhand allows a player to wait until the very last instant before committing himself on these options. Thus what a backhand may lack in power, it more than makes up for in deception and precision.

As with the forehand, the stroke is better if you put underspin on the ball by holding the racquet face open and stroking slightly downward. And like the forehand, the best way to learn it is to go into a court by yourself and hit backhand after backhand to yourself, until you have mastered the control and the length. Don't worry about power. When your timing is right, the ball will zing fast enough. Trying overly hard to put your shoulder into the stroke at the beginning will only cause you to hit the ball off center and at the wrong time. The power you have managed to transmit down the shaft of your racquet will be muted.

SERVES

AND RETURNS

Too often the serve is used merely to put the ball in play rather than as the offensive weapon it should be. True, only a very few players can hit a squash ball hard enough to ace an opponent with any regularity. And three times out of four even these horrendous smashes will bounce up out of the back corner docile as lambs. It's discouraging. So why bother, say some, and the next time they serve up a lob. But if the squash serve does not give a player the overwhelming advantage the tennis serve does, it should give him an edge — and that, after all, is how points are won. There are two basic serves. Variations on these can be used, but they have little more value than to catch a sleepy opponent off guard.

BASIC SERVES

Most players use the lob serve — simply a carefully hit lob, aimed to come back and drop as deep as possible into the back corner of the opposing service box. It should loop as high as the ceiling permits. The more vertical its drop the harder it will be to return.

Because it is always harder to hit a ball that is close to the wall and has just changed direction you should aim the lob serve to glance off the side wall just above your opponent's reach, and at such a point that if he lets it bounce it will be too close to the back wall for him to get his racquet solidly behind it. The ball should hit the side wall, but it should not hit the back wall before it bounces on the floor, because that will send it bouncing out into center court where the receiver can make an easy putaway.

If every lob serve you hit drops the way it should, you will be starting every point you serve at a slight advantage — a margin that between two evenly matched players should make the difference between winning and losing. And there is no reason why even novice players cannot, after a few half-hour practice sessions, get this shot down pat, since it requires only a minimum of technique and there is no element of speed involved.

This is not true of the second basic serve—the slam or hard serve. To be effective this must be hit with devastating power and pinpoint accuracy. But whereas you will rarely win a point outright with a lob serve, a player with a good hard serve can count on several points a game from it. The hard serve is an overhead smash that derives most of its speed from a whiplike crack of the wrist. Ideally, it should rebound from the front wall straight toward the back corner of your opponent's service box so that he cannot be sure whether it is going to strike the back wall or the side wall, and thus will be unable to position himself to anticipate the bounce. In either case, it should hit the back wall before bouncing on the floor, since the bounce will be much lower that way. If you cannot hit the ball hard enough so that it will carry to the back wall on the fly along an almost flat trajectory, don't try the hard serve. But even if you are hitting a hard serve properly, vary it every few times with serves that break off the side wall at about shoulder level and right at the receiver, or hit one straight at him so that he has to jump out of the way or block it back. Also mix in a lob serve from time to time. These may not cause him the same trouble as the hard serve that catches the corner, but they will prevent him from positioning himself and his racquet to volley the ball before it gets there.

The hard serve must be just that—hard enough so that you rush your opponent, causing him to miss altogether or to make a weak return. Not everyone can do that. Moreover, the reaction times of opponents vary greatly. You will find that a hard serve that is effective against one player gives another no trouble at all. If you see you are not particularly hurting your opponent with the hard serve, it is not worth keeping on with it except now and then for variety's sake, because it is tiring to hit. On the other hand, if you feel you are getting a bit sluggish and need a kick in the pants to get going again, hit a few hard serves just to get your adrenalin moving.

RETURNING SERVES

Making the most of your return of a lob serve depends on experience. Since it is easier to move forward than backward, place yourself roughly halfway back in the service box, close to the center line of the court. Face the side wall, but watch the server over your shoulder. Judging the trajectory of his serve, you must make a split-second decision whether to hit the ball on the fly or let it bounce. If it is a good serve, you should volley it just as it comes off the wall. Of course, if you can reach it before it hits the side wall you should do so, dropping it in either corner up front, hitting it deep along your wall, or making a deep cross-court that catches the far wall low down and deep in the back court. Each riposte has its merit, depending on your opponent's strengths and weaknesses, and, of course, depending on what you have done the times before. You must vary the pattern of your play always, whether returning serves or carrying on a rally, so that your opponent cannot guess what is coming.

If the serve looks as though it will bounce well out from the back wall, let it, because that way you will have a good leisurely crack at it, and your opponent will have to move off the T to get out of your way. Some lob serves may be hit too hard and at too sharp an angle into the side wall. Sometimes the only way to play these is by "turning" on the ball, that is, following it around and taking it on your backhand although, say, you were receiving it in your forehand court. It is better, however, to back up ahead of the ball, at the same time backing your opponent off the T and pinning him to the side wall while you have the full court to shoot at.

1

The effectiveness of the hard serve depends on the element of surprise — not surprise that your opponent is hitting a hard serve; his wind-up tips that off in plenty of time; but surprise at the unpredictable jackrabbit bounds the ball takes caroming off the three perpendicular planes — floor, side wall and back wall — that make up the corner of the receiver's box. The best way to prevent this is to volley any serve that stands a chance of reaching the corner. When you see your opponent winding up to smash a serve, take a step or two back. This will give you a split second more time to get your racquet on the ball.

The hard serve produces an infectious tendency in the receiver to slam it back. Resist this. Accuracy is much more important. Hold your racquet out in front of you and meet the ball like a baseball player laying down a bunt, and like a bunt, keep it as close to the base line (the walls) as possible.

2

3

4

5

LOB
VOLLEY
DROP SHOT

● These three strokes have two major points in common. First, they need not be considered special strokes, but rather modifications of the basic backhand and forehand. To the degree that you make each starting with the same basic motions, you will mask your intention and keep your opponent off balance. Second, none of the three shots is used as often as it should be.

THE LOB is essentially a defensive ploy. Use it to gain time to recover when you have been pulled dangerously out of position. Or use it like a baseball pitcher throwing a change-up, to break the rhythm of your opponent's game.

To be effective a lob must be hit high enough so that your opponent cannot hit it from center court no matter how high he reaches. It must move him back and to the side of the T so that you can take that strategic position. Ideally, it should be lofted so that if allowed to bounce it would drop dead in one of the back corners of the court. This will force your opponent to volley it. But he will be making his stroke close to the wall, where it will be hard for him to hit a shot that will press you. It may even force him into a weak return in which case you should be set on the T ready to take advantage of it. Do not, however, expect to win a point outright with a lob. By gaining time for yourself you are also giving your opponent all the time he needs to return it. If he does not, it is his error, not your brilliance.

The lob stroke itself must be made with much less force than a normal ground stroke. Deception is not important. The swing should be slow and precise, with the racquet face well under the ball and the carry-through in the upward direction of the ball's intended flight. The trajectory should take full advantage of the height of the ceiling of the court. This means that in some courts the ball can rise six feet or more above the point it hits high up on the front wall. If there are lights hanging down, don't try to thread the ball between them — reserve that bit of virtuosity for your lob serve, when you are allowed a second try if you miscalculate. In any case, the higher the apex of the trajectory, the more time you have to get back into position.

An added advantage of the high looping lob is that the more vertical the drop, the harder it will be for your opponent to slam the ball back, if so be his wish. Because the timing is less critical, it is always easier to hit a ball back in the same general direction it came from than to alter its course radically to the left or right, or up or down. Thus, it is easier to return a lob with a lob, or a cross-court with a cross-court. A well-executed lob is a safe shot to make, and it can play havoc with an impatient player intent on slamming the tar out of the ball.

A VOLLEY — that is, a stroke that cuts the ball off in midair before it bounces on the floor — is primarily offensive in spirit. It is also used to cut off shots that, if allowed to bounce, would present problems (like the lob that is going to drop into a back corner) and to hold your position in front of your opponent by cutting off his passing shots that might otherwise be taken off the back wall. A volley can be made at any elevation, from just above the floor to well above the shoulder. Still, it follows the basic forehand or backhand pattern of stroke production — with one major exception: being more hurried, it usually begins with a shorter backswing.

THE DROP SHOT is an entirely offensive move. It must be hit at the right time in a rally and with great care, because if it goes even slightly wrong — if it hangs in the air too long, or if it is not close enough to the side wall, or if your opponent is in front of you when you hit it — the other player has a good chance of getting to the ball and winning the point himself. Deception is all important. So begin the stroke as if you were going to drive the ball, only do not follow through. This stopping of your arm at the moment of contact will give a smart snap to the ball while at the same time muting the power of the stroke so that the ball will not carry far after it hits the front wall.

3   . . . to drop the ball . . .

4   . . . for a sure winner up front.

1 A scrambling, weak return . . .

2 . . . presents an opportunity . . .

5 But a full stroke . . .

6 . . . brings the ball back too far.

The walls in squash present special problems and special opportunities. A ball hit high and hard will not, as in tennis, go out of bounds, but it is almost certain to break out into the center of the court, where it becomes a sitting duck. Shots that do not rebound off any but the front wall, yet hug the walls as closely as possible, pulling your opponent off the T and inhibiting his swing, should be the bread and butter of your game. There are, however, some exceptions.

Defensively, there are endless ways to use the walls to return the ball to the front wall from positions where straight shots would be impossible. You will acquire these shots instinctively as you get the feel of the court. The most spectacular is a blast straight into the back wall, made when the ball gets completely past you. If you are quick enough and hit it hard enough and with enough lift, it will carry to the front wall and you will have saved, momentarily, the loss of the point.

Offensively, the walls can be used to create the effect of a drop shot, while your stroke maintains most of the power of a drive. This has the dual effect of fooling your opponent and maintaining the pace of the ball. The most effective shot in this category is the reverse corner shot (diagram 1). Drilled crisply and tightly into the forward corner of the court opposite to the side the ball is hit on — side wall, front wall, floor — a good corner shot is all but unreturnable. The danger is that if the shot is not low enough, it will carry to the opposite wall, rebound, and present an excellent opportunity to your opponent for a kill (diagram 2).

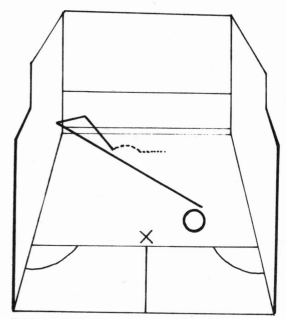

DIAGRAM 1
Reverse corner

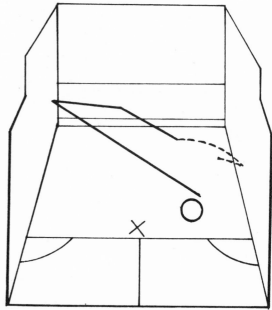

DIAGRAM 2
Reverse corner, muffed

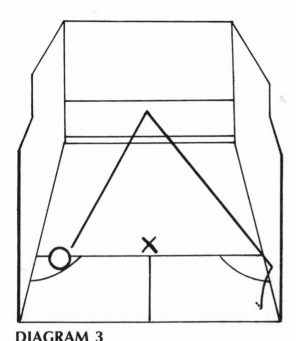

DIAGRAM 3
Cross-court drive

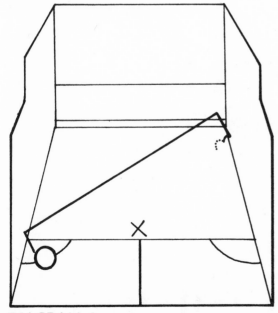

DIAGRAM 4
Boast

A classic ground stroke is the cross-court drive that is hit hard and deep enough to catch the side wall at about the middle of the service box, no higher than a foot above the floor. From there it breaks down to the floor, angling low and obliquely toward the back wall (diagram 3). This is one of the best of all squash shots, because when made properly it stands a good chance to win the point, but when missed it still keeps your opponent in the back of the court.

Any well-hit ball that "nicks" into the crack between the wall and the floor will roll out in such a way as to be all but unplayable. Often this is the only way top-notch, top-shape players can score consistently against one another, and you will see them repeatedly hitting shots intended for the nick. This requires tremendous power and speed afoot, however, for shots that miss the nick by as much as an inch will bounce out and present good targets. The player who goes for them must be ready to cover for his minutest miscalculation.

The boast shot (diagram 4), so named because the player who makes it emphatically signals his virtuosity, may also be considered part of the repertoire of the top player. It enables a player driven deep into the back court (a position where ordinarily he would only be able to hit a ball down the rail or at best a poorly angled cross-court) to drop it dead in the far corner up front. You will learn this one only after hours of practice. But the player who has mastered it wields a devastating weapon.

CAROMS

POSITION AND THE KILL

1 Here begins . . . **2** . . . a 25-frame Wood-Vehslage exchange . . . **3** . . . emphasizing the importance of position.

⬤ Once you have achieved a certain proficiency at putting the ball roughly where you want it when you want to, the game of squash becomes one of position. The key position is the T — the juncture of the perpendicular floor lines that define the service courts. This is the high ground. Hold it and you control the game; relinquish it and you become vulnerable.

An experienced player properly poised on the T is in a commanding position from which he should be able to field all but the most daring or deceptive shots his opponent makes. The exceptions are those exquisite placements that just graze the top of the telltale or hit within inches of the crux of one of the forward corners of the court, or those that are made with such deception that the receiving player is drawn off the T in the wrong direction. But under pressure only superb players can make these shots with any consistency, and ordinarily their competition will be such that the pressure on them will be terrific and the threat of punishment for any less-than-perfect placement will be enough to make them think twice before attempting an overly daring shot. Daring

shots, when they work, are lovely to see. When they fail they are just another blunder.

Nothing is more pleasing, of course, than to snatch victory from the jaws of defeat — and because of the nature of the game of squash this often happens, although not always intentionally. A desperate stab at a ball that is all but by you may send it skittering off the side wall and just barely to the front wall above the telltale, where it drops dead for a winner. It happens, and it happens frequently, but it is not percentage squash. And in the long run it will not win games, because the odds are that your opponent will have his equal share of lucky breaks.

Better, then, to plan to play a steady game in which your shots are aimed safely above the telltale — the definition of "safely" depending on your position on the court and the time you have to make the shot. Obviously, if you are standing 6 feet from the front wall you can aim the ball to hit an inch or two above the telltale and expect success. The same shot made from 30 feet back on the dead run presents another problem.

4 Wood's backhand . . .

5 . . . rail shot . . .

6 . . . stretches Vehslage off the T.

10 . . . the back corner . . .

11 . . . holding the T . . .

12 . . . and forcing a weak return . . .

As soon as you hit a ball — indeed, in the very act of hitting the ball — you should, if you can, be moving back toward the T, getting ready to field your opponent's return. But first you have to earn the right to take the T. Remember that after you hit the ball you may not in any way hinder your opponent from making his return from whatever position he chooses. Thus you cannot take the T if doing so puts you in his direct firing line to the front wall. For one thing, unless you are playing a friendly game and have agreed to take all hits over, which many players do when playing with-out a referee, you lose the point if you are hit with the ball. For another, it hurts like billy-be-damned to be stung with a squash ball traveling upwards of 80 miles per hour. The rules in this regard state that a player has the right to hit the ball to any part of the front wall or near the front wall. To take the T, then, you must place your shot so that it draws your opponent into one of the ex-tremities of the court and leaves you free to move into the center without getting in his way in the process.

7 He lobs poorly...

8 ...to Wood on the T...

9 ...who hits into...

13 ...from which he should...

14 ...make a winner.

15 But he blows it.

The extremities are four — the four corners — plus the space within a few inches of any of the four walls, where a player is unable to hit the ball in the center of his racquet because to do so would mean smashing the frame into the wall. (It happens. When it happens too often or too hard, you will need a new racquet.)

There are certain disadvantages and advantages to playing balls into the front and rear corners. Balls hit into the rear corners, for instance, are covering the greatest straight-line distance in the court, allowing the retrieving player the maximum possible time to field them. Yet, when he does field them he is in the least advantageous position to make a shot that will hurt you. Thus deep shots to either back corner, whether hit up and down the wall or cross-court, are relatively safe shots. Their purpose is to pull your opponent off the T, not to win the point. Balls hit into the forward corners, on the other hand, either as drop shots, corner shots, or boasts, are designed to be winners, but they must be perfectly executed or they become sitting ducks.

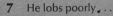

16 Vehslage lobs again . . .

17 . . . this time drawing . . .

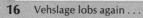

19 . . . to his right . . .

20 . . . where he hits off balance . . .

22 . . . an opportunity . . .

23 . . . to move up front . . .

18 ...Wood back and ...

21 ...giving Vehslage ...

Thus the basic game can be seen as a fencing match, with each player hitting deep shots to draw the other off the T into the back corners, working to force a weak return that he can pounce on up front or cut off in the center of the court. Just when a weak return is weak enough to be taken advantage of is a matter of judgment, depending on a split-second evaluation of your and your opponent's relative skills. But when you do decide to strike, use no half measures. Go for a winner. If you do not quite make it, and your opponent manages to reach the ball, he should at least be pressed so hard that the best he can do is make a defensive return.

There is no more pathetic sight than to see a player who appears to have a decided advantage over another player making the good shots to the back of the court, keeping his opponent off balance and scrambling into the corners, and then becoming impatient and trying for a putaway up front before the opportunity is truly ripe, muffing it, and having his opponent pounce on the ball and win the point. Make your openings with long, safe drives, varying them occasionally with a short shot or two to tire your opponent and to keep him guessing — it's only a step from the center of the court to either side wall; it's three long steps up to the front wall. Then, when the time is right for the putaway, be prepared to take it decisively.

24 ...and ...

25 ...win the point.

Binns/Mo Khan

CONCENTRATION

● Squash is a game of strategy, and strategy depends on concentration. Only by intense concentration can one hope to make the moves that will outwit an opponent. Because of the speed of play and the opportunity — nay, the necessity — for deception, wits mean more than will or way. Over and over again, when watching hard-fought squash matches, you will see first one player surge with a run of points and then the other. This is directly attributable to the intensity of concentration. You may think you are concentrating on the game when actually you are not. You may be letting your mind wander up such unproductive avenues as an appraisal of the score or the dismissal of your opponent's last lucky shot, or you may mentally not even be on the court at all.

If you are going to enjoy, really enjoy, squash and derive the most out of your hour or half hour on the court, you must train your mind as well as your body. You must begin to think like a high-speed computer, evaluating and reevaluating your every move and your opponent's every move in the light of all the play that went before and projecting that into a concept for a series of shots to come. Every exchange will constitute new data to be digested and projected into an appropriately altered plan of action.

When your mind is clicking away like this, while your body is sweating and straining to perform as directed, there can be few sweeter feelings in sport. You are totally immersed — mind and body — in what you are doing, and the rest of the world be damned. This is the real relaxation that squash offers and why it makes such a perfect vehicle for tense office-bound workers to unwind on. Conversely, there is no more frustrating feeling than to know that technically, physically, you are hitting the ball as well as you are able but losing point after point. It happens because your concentration is faltering. You are, in fact, only half there.

Sharif Khan

ADVANCED TACTICS

● Volumes could be written on the nuances, variations, and imaginative sequences of shots with which two top-notch players prod and probe for chinks in each other's armor. But the major difference between the tactics used by everyday players and those who play more seriously boils down to a few basic concepts or ways of looking at the game.

There is a strong tendency, for instance, for the everyday squash player to play the game one stroke at a time. When it is his turn to hit the ball he comes alive, dashes to position, and makes as strong a shot as he is able. But then — mentally, at any rate — he pauses, becomes a spectator, waiting to see what his opponent's riposte will be. When that becomes clear, with the ball already coming at him off the front wall, he picks up play again. This, of course, is a great exaggeration, but it does describe the mind-set of most average players more closely than a description of how each stroke *ought* to be considered — that is, as interlocking building blocks that together make a point.

Ideally, each point should be played as a series of shots aimed toward maneuvering one's opponent into a position from which eventually he will be unable to reach your next shot. This would be easy enough to do if it were not for the fact that he is intent upon the same course and will be constantly frustrating your plans, snatching away, as it were, your blocks as fast as you lay them up. Thus the combinations you try must be flexible and you must constantly be willing to go back to the drawing board, undiscouraged, and start over. Patience in most things is a virtue. In squash it is a necessity.

If squash is a game of position, like chess, it is also a game of percentages, stamina, and timing. It would be hard to argue that a player presented with the opportunity to make a certain winning shot should not take it. However, such choices seldom present themselves so neatly. More often, the proposition will be something like this.

Your opponent hits a screeching cross-court. The angle is not perfect, however, and with a quick forward lunge you can cut it off, as you should. But at this point you have a choice — to bang it hard, high, and safe into the back corner, or to try to drop it up front for a winner. If you opt for the winner, you have roughly a 25 percent chance of making it and about the same chance of forcing a weak return. On the other hand, you have a 25 percent chance of allowing your opponent to make a return that will put you on the defensive and a 25 percent chance that you will muff the shot altogether and lose the point right then and there. If, instead, you hit deep, you have almost no chance of winning the point, but a 25 percent chance of forcing your opponent into a weak return and a 75 percent chance that you will simply be maintaining the ball in play without permitting your opponent any special advantage.

If you go for the drop shot, the odds are 50-50 that you will win or lose the point, either then and there, or in the long run. In other words, you gain nothing. If you try the second shot, you will gain an advantage one time out of four — and at no appreciable risk. Obviously this is the better choice. But the difference between the ordinary player and the top player is that the former, if he thinks he has a chance, will try the first shot most of the time, while the latter will opt for the shot that gives him the edge on percentage — most of the time. There are exceptions, like the finale of the Ufford-Adair contest, when Ufford chose the precisely right moment to break the pattern and win the match.

I have said that it would be hard to argue against ending a point when the opportunity presented itself; but now I am going to. It may pay you in the long run to keep a point going, keeping the pressure on your opponent, running him down. Of course, he may get lucky and win the point that you have purposely prolonged, but eventually your investment should pay off — providing his stamina is not greater than yours.

The fourth dimension used by good players is timing. By that I do not mean the timing that makes a beautifully executed shot, but the fact that every squash point, game, and match has, as it unfolds, a past, present, and future. The player who is most keenly aware of this has a strong advantage. Just as a good player should be looking ahead and planning the flow of his shots, he must also look back at the sequence of shots both he and his opponent has made. What are his opponents' weaknesses, what sequences does his opponent favor that he can anticipate, what sequences has he himself used and should therefore vary at some crucial point to foil his opponent's anticipation? These are the questions a serious player should always be asking himself — not in words, there is no time for that, but in some sort of mental shorthand that for lack of a better word is called experience.

● The rules of squash are most explicit on the physical side — who may move where, when, with what, and to what purpose. They are all but mute on the psychological aspects of the game. And in that broad free-fire zone there is plenty of opportunity for personal expression. It is there that the "gamesman," to use Stephen Potter's famous term, finds room to maneuver.

Whatever ploy the gamesman uses, his aim is to rattle his opponent, to make him lose his cool. Because squash requires such intense concentration and because the players compete at such close quarters, the opportunities for uncooling an opponent are endless.

The question is, should you play that way? Squash is traditionally billed as a gentleman's game — which means, I suppose, that you should bend over backward to give your opponent every legitimate break. Certainly, if both players bend equally far, they produce the ideal game.

But, I find that attitude a touch too simon-pure. If, for instance, I discover that the man in the court with me is severely out of breath, I hold it only right and proper to keep the pressure on him by not dawdling over my serve. Whereas if I am dragging around the court like an empty sack, I see no reason to trot back to the server's box at the end of every point. A measured pace will do. And on occasion it does not hurt if you purposely hit your first serve out of bounds, giving you another few seconds to catch your breath.

Another example: You are playing without a referee (all the remarks that follow assume the absence of a referee) and your opponent has returned a ball that you thought bounced twice. Do you challenge him or not? Perhaps the most gentlemanly thing would be to ignore the infraction — in fact, most people do just that most of the time, because to call someone on a double bounce is a

GAMESMANSHIP

direct challenge to his integrity, a sort of slap in the face. However, if you are sure — very sure — of your ground, you should tell him that you thought it was a double bounce. For, either he is oblivious to his mistake, in which case he should be perfectly willing to play the point over, or he knows he has cheated, in which case he is symbolically slapping *you* in the face — and no gentleman ordinarily declines that challenge. If that does not produce a change in his style of play you can simply decline to play with him in the future, or if you find you must play him in a tournament you should ask for a referee. Even if you cannot get one, the act of asking should itself stand as an embarrassing rebuke.

As for the styles of gamesmen who operate within the letter if not within the spirit of the rules, the range of their invention defies description. However, in my experience all fall into three general categories. To define these categories I will have to admit to a currently unpopular concept. In my mind each of the three types is represented by a national stereotype as portrayed by Hollywood in the hundreds of movies I absorbed like a great adolescent sponge during the decade of the '40s. There is first the storm trooper — Helmut Dantine, perhaps, or Walter Slezak in *Lifeboat*. As the match begins, he points to the dried splotch of blood on the floor and says he hopes you are better at keeping out of his way than the last fellow he played in that court. If his swing turns out to be as gauche as his opening remark, and his style of play demands more *Lebensraum* than you care to give him, tell him so. If he persists, walk off the court — preferably in the middle of a point, suggesting as you duck through the door that you would be glad to play again when he learns how. I recommend such an exit even if it means defaulting an important match—better by far to lose a match than your front teeth.

Second is the insidious Dr. Fu Manchu, the one who smiles knowingly as he stabs you in the back. I know one player flagrant in this ploy — and I have to admit he drives me up the wall. He hits, for instance, a beautifully executed shot that a 20-year-old Hashim Khan could not have reached, and as he picks up the ball, tentatively, as if he should really be handing it back to you, he comes out with a remark such as "Oh, bad luck, you were right on top of it," or "How lucky can I get?" or "Sorry, take a let" — implying that he was in your way, whereas he was actually on the other side of the court. The only real remedy for this is to accept the let. This is an affront to one's dignity — as he well knows — but all I can recommend is to grit your teeth and bear it. But don't grit them too hard or it will throw off your swing.

The third type is equally hard to handle. He is the Russian chest beater — polite and proper toward you, but an absolute Rasputin when it comes to his own play. You hit, for instance, the same marvelous shot that Dr. Fu Manchu executed in the last example. Rasputin lunges for it — doesn't come close — and the next thing you hear is a volley of terrible self-directed oaths that would bring a blush to the cheeks of a chief boatswains mate. A few points later he misses again and a note of hysteria creeps into his bellow. He is an incompetent ape, he stinks, he is an uncoordinated gluefooted geriatric patient whose moves are glacial. And so it goes at top voice until, if you are not careful, you begin to believe what he is saying and, being human, let up a little — who, after all, would play his hardest against a "spastic basket case." Before you know it you have lost the match.

The proper riposte for this type is to play the oversolicitous Dr. Fu Manchu to his Rasputin, until he becomes so infuriated at you that he forgets to concentrate on his own woes. In which case you may win the match but lose a future opponent.

And that, now that I think of it, is the ultimate and just reward visited upon all successful gamesmen.

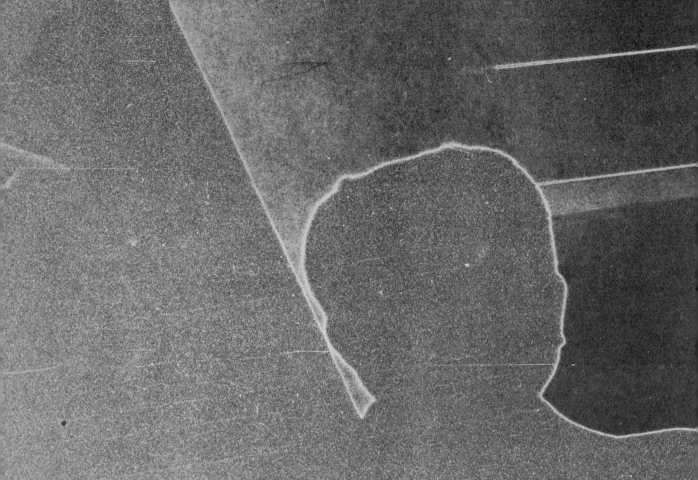

WORLD SQUASH

THE INTERNATIONAL GAME

Around 1970, with an eye toward the 1976 Olympics slated for Montreal, a movement arose to effect a compromise between the British game of squash rackets and the dialect played in North America. The purpose was to create a middle ground where the two divisions of the squash world — the North American Continent, and everywhere else on earth where squash is played — could vie with one another on roughly equal footing.

Although the basic theory governing each game is identical, the differences go deeper than the spelling of "racket" and "racquet." The top players at the British form of the game, for instance, are caught flatfooted by the speed of our heavier, harder, and more lively ball, while the best American players can hardly score a point against well-conditioned British players when using their ball and playing on their court, which is two and a half feet wider than ours.

At this writing, the attempt at compromise, called the international game, still is in the testing stage. The question of court size — most knotty of all because of the expense involved in altering the dimensions of existing courts — has been shelved temporarily. Whatever court is available is used. Actually, the greater width of the British court is largely compensated for by the fact that the top of the American telltale, at 17 inches, is two inches lower than the English telltale. American scoring is used, in which every point counts toward game score, rather than as in the British system in which only the server can score toward game. The ball, which is the major difference between the two games, is the one developed in Australia. Called, with customary Aussy restraint, the Australian Yellow Dot Extra Super Slow, it is slow only in relation to the American ball; actually, it is a slightly souped-up version of the British ball. It weighs less than the American ball and can be — and usually is — played with the lighter and more supple British racquet, atlhough this choice is up to the player.

A leading proponent of the international game is the British Open Champion Jonah Barrington, an enterprising and highly energetic young English professional who sees it as a means to liberate squash from the upper-class men's clubs on both sides of the Atlantic, where for over a century this potentially lusty, gutsy game has been held captive and aloof from the masses. Evidence that the release would be welcome abounds in Australia, where on public squash courts throughout the country one is equally apt to see plumbers and truck drivers, their wives and children, playing the game as stock brokers and organization men. Despite the Australians' boundless enthusiasm for sports in general and racquet sports in particular, this proliferation of the sport down under would probably not have happened on the scale that it has if they had been playing the American game, because the heavy American ball requires a more ruggedly constructed court.

But if squash is to gain the true popularity that Barrington believes it deserves, another element must be added — the spectator.

Jonah Barrington   photo: Bob Lehman

Until recently, the question of whether squash, like tennis, had a wide appeal for audiences outside the ranks of those who play or played the game themselves was purely academic. The largest gallery in the world — in Peshawar, Pakistan, home of the legendary Khan family, which is to squash racquets what the Zacchini family is to being shot from cannons — accommodates a mere 600 spectators, and most court galleries are considered large if they seat more than 50. What this means to professionals like Barrington and the Khans is that there is no money to be made playing the game before a paying audience, even if it turns out to draw like a combination of wrestling, football, and blue movies. Traditionally, squash professionals have earned their living by teaching, stringing racquets, and being generally available to play with club members who need a game. When a professional travels to play in a tournament it is purely to enhance or maintain his reputation and not for the money — travel expenses plus a crack at the winner's and runner-up's purses, which seldom amount to more than a few hundred dollars.

Presently, however, the development of tough, see-through plastics — like those used for basketball backboards — promises the possibility of manufacturing a portable court that could be set up in any large arena for thousands to watch, while television could in turn bring the game into millions of living rooms. This is the dream that excites the likes of Barrington and Sharif Khan, the present standardbearer of the Khan clan, whose eyes take on a certain faraway glint when they are reminded of the $10,000-a-night performances that tennis stars like Rod Laver are turning in with increasing frequency.

But if, as they foresee, squash is ripe for benevolent exploitation, they want to make sure that they make their initial pitch with as marketable a product as possible. From the point of view of the spectator, fault can be found with both the American and the British games. What these shortcomings boil down to is that the American ball travels almost too fast for the naked eye to follow — certainly too fast for the television eye. The points are often over almost before they start, and the spectator is left with little more to build suspense than to watch the score mount. The British ball, on the other hand, is too slow. The players are kept constantly moving, to be sure, but points can last for minutes at a time. Games, under their scoring, can seesaw back and forth for hours. A spectator can leave the gallery to get a drink and come back ten minutes later and have missed nothing. Stamina, more than skill, is the prime requisite for winning.

The international game is designed to eliminate these drawbacks, while keeping the best of both games. In the spring of 1971, when Barrington and Sharif Khan came to town in their roles as promoters to give an exhibition, some of us in New York who had been experimenting, largely in the dark, with the international ball were afforded the pleasure of seeing how the hybrid version ought to be played.

On a sunny Sunday afternoon — the first of the spring season, when any New Yorker with sense would have been outdoors under the cherry blossoms across the street in Central Park — some thirty aficionados of squash, myself included, packed the low-ceilinged gallery of the New York

Athletic Club courts. What we saw was an exhibition of speed, acrobatics, endurance, timing, and teeth-gritting will for which I know no apt analogy in sport. The will, endurance, and close man-on-man confrontation are likened to boxing by Barrington, who trains accordingly, with roadwork, exercises, and hours spent in the court by himself perfecting his shots, both with and without a ball. The speed and acrobatics are probably unique.

When the match was over — Sharif, possibly because he was more used to the narrower court than Barrington, eked out a suitably close five-game victory — and the hat was passed to pay for the players' expenses, I doubt if there was a spectator in the gallery who was not thoroughly convinced that however much he loved his own brand of squash, this, or something very like it, was the game of the future.

Because the ball moved more slowly, the players were able to hurtle around the court running down shots and slamming other shots that would have been impossible with the longer-bounding American ball. To compensate for this squashy ball, they wound up with lashlike strokes that made the air hiss as the racquet rent it. Thus struck, the ball attained nearly the speed of the American ball. Smacking the front wall, it flattened into a pancake shape and with the air compressed to nothing inside it literally exploded off the front wall with firecracker bangs.

I watched, I wondered, and evidently I learned. The next time I played with the international ball with a friend who had regularly been winning drinks from me whenever we played, I beat him badly. Unfortunately, in doing so I evidently passed along much of what I had acquired, for on our next go, I signed the bar bill as usual. The moral of this story is that one can learn a lot simply from watching others — both good and bad.

Indeed, if there is a hortatory theme to this book it is just that. Watch other players — either in the pictures here presented or on the courts — and learn from their brillance and from their mistakes. You must practice what you learn, of course, for there is no other way of fixing what you understand in your repertoire to be available instantly and instinctively. That is your homework. But the lectures will come to you through your eyes. And the better the player, the better the lesson. The best of all are the Khans.

For more than six hours straight on a snowy Saturday in Toronto, I have watched the world's top contenders — professional and amateur — pound a hard rubber ball against the white walls of a wooden room to determine, under the rules governing the American version of squash racquets, who can do it best. At cocktails afterwards and at a dinner dance at Toronto's Badminton and Racquet Club, host to the 1971 North American Open Singles Championship, I have talked, listened, eaten, drunk, and danced squash.

Now, on Sunday morning, to cop a phrase from Christopher Isherwood, I am a camera — a squash-satiated, zoom-lens, instant-replay, slow-motion, stop-action, bipedal camera — poised above the center court, one foot on the rail, one on a seat reserved for the press, looking down, zoomed in close. Projected somewhere inside my skull is the frozen image, platonic in its perfection, of a slightly squashed black ovoid fitting as if molded into parabolic pocket of stretched strings. So tightly does the ball press against the webbing of cream-white sheep gut that its hard rubber surface rises like blisters through the quarter-inch grid. Now the camera angle widens to include a round, laminated ash frame precisely centered on the ball. Wider still, it shows a stout shaft of the same material bent in a shallow curve and clutched in a dark-skinned fist. From the heel of the fist — a left fist — protrudes two-thirds of a leatherbound handle.

The camera will draw back farther still, and in a moment there will be action, but already enough has been recorded for aficionados like the two-hundred spectators packing the gallery beside me to recognize the hand that has already won this world championship five times.

How do they know whose hand it is? Elementary.

First: The depth and symmetry of the indentation that the ball has made in the strings bespeaks a stroke of uncommon power and precision. Perhaps no more than a dozen hands are capable of such virtuosity. Nearly half of these, however, are dark-skinned — among them the hand of the 1969 and 1970 U.S. Amateur Champion, Anil Nayar of India. The others, however, all belong to men called Khan, members of a fabuolus squash dynasty with roots in a single Pakistani city of 100,000, but with branches that reach throughout the world — from squash clubs in Seattle to London, from Bombay to Detroit. Those like Nayar and the Khans who have learned British squash as played east of Suez have a tendency to hold their racquets high up on the handle, as this racquet is being held.

Second: The stroke in question is being made by a left-handed player. Nayar (who, as it happens, is not even competing in this tournament because of a skiing injury) is right-handed; so are all but one of the Khans active in North America. The exception is thirty-one-year-old Mohibullah Khan, who, when he is not traveling to defend the family honor, presides over the fourteen singles courts and one doubles court at the Harvard Club of Boston.

So there you have it. And, as if to confirm the answer, the incredible camera that is me flashes a full shot of the player from the front. He is of medium build, swarthy and classically handsome — square-jawed, with black curly hair and eyes of the same black, eyes that at this instant are riveted on the ball. On the left breast of his white shirt in red letters are the words "Harvard Club, Boston, Mo Khan."

THE
PROFESSIONALS

And now — slowly, slowly at first, because no eye can follow this — the picture begins to move. The strings in the racquet straighten, then bulge outward. The wrist, pivot of power, breaks, causing the dark skin to bunch over taut tendons. Like a lunar landing module undocking in space, the ball moves forward with a slow underspin away from the racquet. It follows a flat trajectory parallel to the floor and a bare 18 inches above it. Mohibullah Khan, who has managed to transfer with maximum efficiency all the motion and power of his muscular body into that single small black sphere, is extended now, not in the classic follow-through of a tennis player, but with the left foot thrust far forward like a left-handed pitcher who has just delivered a fast ball. He finishes his stroke with the racquet head out in front of him and recoils instinctively toward the strategic center of the court.

He need not have. For now, at full speed, we see the result of his shot, since only at full speed can one appreciate how hopeless it is for his opponent to do more than watch the black smudge the ball becomes as it streaks to the front wall, hitting a bare millimeter above the 17-inch-high metal telltale, rebounding half the length of the 32-foot court before skidding briefly on the floor, lifting an inch or two, and touching down again just before striking the rear wall — all in a split second.

Outside the cavern of my mind, platonic absolute becomes reality. Loud applause rises in the gallery around me. But the point, so emphatic in its ending, so evocative of the brand of squash the Khans play, is not decisive. Enough to send the game into extra points, it does not stem the tide that already is lapping dangerously high around Mohibullah's flanks. His opponent, thirty-six-year-old Ken Binns, has the look in all but size (5'11", 180 pounds) of an Anglican choirboy. And today he is hitting all the high notes right on key. Binns has been playing the American game only since 1967, when he immigrated to Canada from Australia, where he had been both a tennis and squash star. He is presently the squash professional at the Skyline Club in Toronto, and each year he has been chipping away at the monolithic wall of Khans that circles the top of the professional squash ladder. Up to this point, however, he has never actually beaten a Khan in a major match, but on several occasions he has forced Mohibullah to the maximum five games.

Now, after Mohibullah with his signature shot has tied the score at 13-all in the fourth game of their semi-final round match, Binns once more forces the contest to the ultimate fifth game, with a virtuoso performance of daring placements that are too much even for the lightning-fast Pakistani. The crowd, sensing an upset, is enraptured, and as the two professionals leave the court through the small door in the rear wall, there is an audible rubbing of hands over what is to come. The players now have two minutes to catch their breaths and mentally prepare themselves for the game that will decide which one of them will proceed to the finals scheduled for three o'clock that afternoon.

photo: B. Swett

Waiting for Mohibullah in the anteroom under the stands is his uncle Hashim Khan, a man whom a knowledgeable sports writer has called the "greatest athlete for his age the world has ever seen" — and before you dismiss that statement as wild journalistic hyperbole, harken unto the facts. First, look at him — not as he is standing now, in slacks and Harris-tweed jacket, talking in rapid Pushtu to his sweating nephew — but in his work clothes: sneakers, socks, shorts, and polo shirt, all white, as specified in the rules of squash, save for the gold-banded watch on his left wrist. With the watch he times the lessons he gives — four dollars for a half hour — at the Uptown Athletic Club in Detroit, where he is the club professional. Hashim Khan is short — 5'4" — and carries under a barrel chest a fair-sized paunch, which Prince Philip in the course of presenting awards at one of the seven British Open tournaments that Hashim won between the years 1950 and 1957 characterized as "quite a tummy." Since his limbs look wiry still, rather than powerful, the tummy must account for the lion's share of his rise in weight from the 112 pounds of more than a quarter of a century ago, when he played in and won his first major tournament, to his present 150 pounds. His features are large, dominated by a big triangular nose with a pronounced bridge. All that is left of his hair is a close-cropped, graying fringe around his ears and the back of his head. The trace of a muddy bruise shows in the soft skin under his right eye, and a jagged purple scar underlies the hairs of his eyebrow, marking the place where a student caught him with a racquet a week or two earlier.

Sharif/Hashim

There is that about Hashim that reminds one strongly of Picasso. There is the physical resemblance. Both men are short, dark, and bald and have piercing eyes. But more than that; one is influenced by the knowledge that the master squash player has changed his style as often and dominated his field as completely as the master painter has his — and for nearly as long. One feels no more need to suspend "Khan" to the former's name than to append "Pablo" to the latter's.

To understand Hashim, one must understand the circumstance into which he was born — and to understand that is to understand the Khan clan, for although Hashim is unique, his uniqueness is one of quantity, not kind.

Hashim was born about the time of the outbreak of World War I, in the small hamlet of Nawakille, near the Khyber Pass. His people were originally Pathan tribesmen from the mountains between Afghanistan and Pakistan. A fifteen-minute walk from Nawakille over dirt roads is the garrison city of Peshawar, then in India — at the time there was no Pakistan. The British army was there in force to guard the pass, and since nothing came through the pass in those days, they, the officers at any rate, took their sports very seriously — polo, pig sticking, tennis, hard racquets, and squash — anything to keep a fellow fit.

In Peshawar, as in other garrison cities throughout India, there already was established a tradition of native professionals, who would take care of the facilities, string racquets, and play with the officers when asked — originally men with long beards and polite manners who tailored their game to humor the British raj, and whose prowess must go forever unrecorded, for there were no tournaments open to professionals in those days. As jobs went in colonial India, however, theirs was a good one, and they passed on both their skills and their prerogatives to their sons, of which these polygamous Moslems had plenty.

The mighty river of squash-playing Khans is traceable to two main sources in Peshawar: Rehmatullah Khan, the imam or prayer leader of the city, and Muhammad Ali. Both these patriarchs lived to be well over ninety. Both also had sons, grandsons, and great-grandsons, too numerous to detail, who are or have been professionals, not only at squash, but also at tennis, hard racquets, and even horse racing, a few with the slight build of Hashim having been noted jockeys in Bombay. Those descendants of Muhammad Ali through the male line, of course, are not Khans but Alis. But Muhammad had a daughter who married a certain Aziz Khan, no relation to Rehmatullah, which is how that name appears in his branch of the family. When a Khan grandson of Muhammad Ali married a Khan granddaughter of Rehmatullah, the two tributaries were united. This merger took

place at about the same time Hashim was born — into yet a third family of Khans. Hashim's father, although an accomplished tennis player, did not belong to a line of professional athletes. Better than that, he was chief steward of the British Army Officers' Club in Peshawar, and through him Hashim at a tender age had the run of the facilities there.

Hashim remembers clearly when, barefoot and wide-eyed, he approached the outdoor courts of the club, climbed the steps, and peered down into the mysterious white room. Later he would spend hours on the walls watching the game being played and running to retrieve the ball when it popped out of the court.

Why Hashim chose squash as his metier rather than tennis or rather than becoming a jockey must remain somewhat of a mystery. But why squash chose Hashim over all the other dark-skinned children across the length and breadth of the Empire to win the British Open an incredible and surely never to be equaled seven times is plain as day: He made it happen. When the courts were empty in the evenings because it was too dark for the officers to see the ball, he played with the sons of other club employees; he played by moonlight; and when at the age of twelve he quit school, after his father had been killed in an accident at the Club, he played Hashim against Hashim in the mornings when the officers were on duty.

Squash, as he says in the biographical chapter of his entertaining book on how to play the game (*Squash Racquets, the Khan Game*, by Hashim Khan with Richard E. Randall, Wayne State University Press, Detroit, 1967), was his whole life. Soon he became proficent enough to be coached by the son of the club professional, grandson of the legendary Rehmatullah. And then he was beating his teacher and could give any of the

British officers a fine customer's game, beating them, but by just a slim enough margin so they would want to play with him again.

Hashim's family had been awarded a pension from the club — enough for his mother and her four children to live on, but no more. Hashim's life settled into a routine not unlike that of a caddy at a large golf club. He would play squash — or tennis or hard racquets — whenever a member needed an opponent, or a partner in doubles. Finally, in 1942 he was offered, and readily accepted, the job of squash professional at the Air Force Officers Mess in Peshawar, with a salary of 50 rupees (about $20) a month — enough to get married on. As is customary in that part of the world, the marriage was arranged by the families of the bride and groom. Evidentally the arrangement was a happy one, since Mehria has born Hashim five daughters and seven squash-playing sons. Mehria herself has never in her life seen the game played, since, even in Detroit, the Khans remain devout Moslems for whom the woman's place is strictly in the home. Hashim's allegiance to the teachings of Muhammed is evidenced in his neither smoking nor drinking, strictures that undoubtedly have contributed to his longevity as a star.

Five years before Hashim's marriage, his sister married one of his squash-playing pals, Safirullah Khan, another grandson of Rehmatullah. Thus Hashim's family was united with the rest of the Khan clan. The most notable squash-playing product of the union of Safirullah and Hashim's sister — but by no means the only one — is the left-handed Mohibullah.

In Toronto, half a world and a third of a century away from the place and time of Mohibullah's birth, Hashim sends his nephew back into the court with a last word and an affectionate slap on the back. "What did you tell him?" someone asks.

"I tell him, hit hard, don't hit tin," answers Hashim, smiling.

Good advice, but not good enough. In the fifth game Mohibullah does not hit the tin often. But he does not hit hard either — that is, not hard for a Khan. Only a few of his shots have the terrible pace of the one that tied the score at 13-all in the fourth game, and given that split-second of grace, Ken Binns weaves a daring game of caroms, hair-splitting drop shots, and drives that hug the wall so close that Mohibullah cannot return them off the center of his racquet, where his power lies. Perhaps he is tired, perhaps he does not care quite enough. Has he not, after all, won the U.S. Open five times? And it is not as though the title is in any danger of passing out of the family, for in the other half of the draw is last year's Open winner, twenty-six-year-old Sharif Khan, Hashim's eldest son and the present standardbearer of the clan. So the thirty-one-year-old Mohibullah lets the game and the match slip away from him, and afterward in the locker room muses somewhat edgily, "Well, you can't win them all."

Mo bumps Binns

At thirty-one, Hashim had barely begun his career — although it is difficult to pinpoint exactly where he was in it, since no one, not even Hashim, who contradicts himself on the subject in his own book, seems to agree on exactly how old he was then or is now. With no official records to go on, the safest assumption one can make — and the one, incidentally, that makes his insurance premiums the lowest — is that he was born in 1916. The reason that assumption is the safest is that of all the conflicting claims, 1916 makes him the youngest, and thus makes the statistics that follow, if not entirely believable, at least more so than they would be if, as some contend — his son Sharif included — Hashim was born sometime before 1911 and is now in his sixties. But never mind his exact age; when he was in his thirties, unlike Mohibullah, he was winning them all. In fact, from 1944, when he was twenty-eight or so and went to Bombay for the first time to compete in the All India tournament, until 1956, when he turned forty, he won every major tournament he entered. It is notable that the end of that incredible twelve-year splurge came in the finals of the British Open at the hands of Hashim's cousin, Roshan Khan, a great-grandson of Muhammad Ali. Hashim was one game up on his way to winning that most prestigious of all world squash titles for the seventh consecutive time when he suffered leg cramps and dropped the next three games and the match.

Hashim's last try at the British Open was in 1959. He was forty-three or so, and in the semifinals with this younger brother Azam, whom he had forcefully converted from a tennis to a squash player, he twisted his knee and had to default. Azam then beat Roshan in the finals, and later went on to win the British Open three more times — proving Hashim to be as adroit a teacher as he was a player. Azam himself has taught a whole generation of young British players from his post at the New Grampian's Sports Club in West London.

Hashim

By the late 1950s and early '60s, the British had become well accustomed to sending their silverware back to Pakistan in the hands of men called Khan. But in 1950, the year that Hashim first appeared out of the East like his namesake Genghis, the impact was comparable to that of a Japanese baseball team sweeping the World Series. Reports that preceded him had been given about as much credence as if they had concerned the Abominable Snowman. What had this fellow Khan done, after all? Won the All-India title a few times? But that was years ago. Now he was an old man of thirty-four. Generally overlooked in England was the fact that the man whom Hashim had beaten in the finals of the All-India tournament in 1944, 1945, and 1946 was none other than his cousin Abdul Bari, who, in 1949, on his first try, had reached the finals of the British Open.

It was just this fact that was *not* overlooked in Karachi, where Bari's exceptional showing had occasioned mixed emotions of pride and consternation — pride because Bari, a great-grandson of Muhammad Ali, was a Pakistani; and consternation, because, in his capacity as squash professional at the Bombay Cricket Club, he was representing India. In 1947, when Great Britain granted independence to its largest colony, India and Pakistan had elected to go their separate ways, and the rivalry between the Hindu and the Moslem states was intense. It was suggested to Bari by the Pakistani High Commissioner in England that next year he represent his true homeland; but that would have meant his giving up his job at the Bombay Cricket Club. And this he was not willing to do.

And then someone thought of Hashim, who since partition had dropped effectively out of competitive play, but was still at his post teaching pilots how to keep fit — only now the pilots belonged to the Royal Pakistani Air Force. The new country, nursing a fierce inferiority complex, was desperate both for exportable commodities and world recognition. An air ticket was inveigled from certain government officials who had hardly heard of the sport, a kitty of $1,000 was raised from among the officers of the mess, and off Hashim went at the age of thirty-four or so to meet the best players in the world in a sport that, far more than the American brand, is known as a young man's game because it requires such stamina.

When Hashim returned three months later he was a national hero — the Pakistani Charles Lindbergh. Overnight, squash became the most popular game in the country. Public courts were erected in many cities. Today, Peshawar fittingly boasts a court with one of the two largest galleries in the world, able to accommodate some 600 spectators. Eventually, after repeating his performance several times in England, Hashim was awarded a special purse from the government of 10,000 rupees plus 60 acres of prime farm land. The railway depot near Nawakille was renamed Hashim Khan's Village, and he was gazetted a lieutenant in the RPAF, the only Pakistani officer with neither high school nor college degree. "This is not proper," said Merza Secunder, who signed the decree, "but we do this for Hashim."

As an emissary of the Pakistan government he traveled all over the world putting on exhibitions. In one week in Australia and New Zealand he played 350 games. During the 1950s, his fame spread, and by the time he decided to retire from active competition in the British game after twisting his knee and having to default to his brother, he was the most famous squash player in the world. Little wonder, then, that the U.S.A., with its penchant for importing the best the world has to offer, had to have him. And Hashim, in turn, had to have America, where, because our version of squash requires less running and more racquet work, he might prolong his career by several decades.

Hashim and Roshan Khan warm up for finals of 1956 North American Open. Hashim won.

photo: Bob Lehman

He had come a long way since that British Open, back in 1950, when on his first sojourn abroad, with only a minimal command of English, he had met the Egyptian professional and reigning champion, Mahmoud El Karim. Here, in part, is Hashim's description of that historic match:

"Never before do I see a man like this in squash racquets. He is higher than six feet, long arms and legs, and he moves about the court like I see dancer in ballet, soft and smooth, you never hear his feet on the floor, and how he turns and runs and strokes, you want to watch all day, it is wonderful. He is what one calls a stroke player, his play has rhythm, no jerks. And he has many different shots, some I see for the first time anywhere.

"My game is simple at this time. I drive very hard and low, cross-court, and sometimes I play a soft drop shot, that is all. But speed on my feet I have this, I can get to ball. Also I think fast. When I am up front in court and El Karim tries to pass me with ball, sometimes I surprise him: I do not run after that ball to back, I leap out and get that ball in front. Ball is going very fast, yes, but I see that ball clear, I have time to think about this ball and where I must leap and where I must place it.

"When games are finished" — three straight, two of them without Karim winning a single point — "a British professional tells me, 'Many times you play off wrong foot.' Quite right. This is when I must stroke in an instant. If I turn to face side wall, ball does not wait for me. I know it is not proper, it is bad style, it is not nice to see, it is a mistake. But sometimes it wins points."

Not surprisingly, that description fits like a glove the final of the North American Open played twenty-one years later in Toronto between Binns and Hashim's son Sharif, who, although five inches taller, looks hauntingly like pictures of his father at the outset of his career — lean, dark-browed, with intense eyes.

Sharif

One wonders about these eyes. Always it seems the question comes up in club lounges when the Khans are mentioned: what is it that makes them so much better than everyone else. The logical answer, of course, is practice. Hashim, virtually from the time he could first hold a racquet, has devoted all his waking hours to squash. And I daresay he sleeps it, too. But logical answers are not what are wanted in these discussions, which tend toward the mystical. Someone will suggest that the Moslem diet is the secret, or the fact that these men learned the game in Peshawar, at an altitude of 1,113 feet, and now play at sea level. I say it is the eyes, which are, after all, the key to racquet sports. And I cite for scripture Hashim's description of his first match with El Karim — "ball is going very fast, yes, but I see that ball clear ..."

This Toronto match, of course, is being played according to the American rules and with the American ball, which moves even faster than the English ball. Sharif has been practicing with it for only the past week. Before that, he was with Jonah Barrington and two other professionals putting on exhibitions of the English game throughout the world. He has left the tour to defend his North American Title. Because the English game requires much more stamina, he is in superb shape, but his touch, so necessary for the delicate soft shots, is not all it might be. He makes up for this by melting the ball with power strokes of the sort his cousin Mohibullah needed more of in his fifth game with Binns.

Sharif has reached the finals by destroying the amateur Larry O'Loughlin in straight games. At one point, toward the end of their match, O'Loughlin, a powerful hitter in his own right, let his racquet get away from him. There was a splintering crash at the front wall and the thing dropped in a heap on the floor, the frame crushed and bent, the shaft broken in two. Sharif picked it up gingerly in cupped hands, as he might a wounded bird. The symbolism in his handing the wreckage to O'Loughlin was unmistakable: Sorry, Sharif was saying, but this is what I do to games like yours.

With Binns, a better player than O'Loughlin, the result is no different. Twice, Sharif runs the big Australian right out of his shoe — literally. When it happens for the second time, Binns changes to a brand-new pair of sneakers and squeaks around the court like a rusty hinge — only there is nothing rusty about his movements. Next to the Khans, he is the best there is at the American game. It is just that he cannot move fast enough to keep up with Sharif's power. Three and four times a game he is actually hit by the serve coming off the back wall.

After it is over, sitting with friends in the Badminton and Racquet Club bar — but not drinking himself, nor smoking as Binns is; that much of his Moslem heritage stays with him — Sharif discusses the match.

"I'm out to win. At first I was out to impress all those 'splendid chaps.' " He pronounces the last words in a derisive, super-upper-class British accent. He is referring to the nine years he spent on an athletic scholarship at a British boarding school. "I did everything right, but I didn't win." Not entirely true, since he won a number of junior British championships in those years. "Now I just play a trash game. I'm lucky to have good wrists and a good eye." There, you see, the eyes again!

Hashim, who is about to drive back to Detroit with some of his admirers from the Uptown Athletic Club, comes by for a quick word with Sharif. Since he still is traveling a lot, Sharif asks his father to take back home for safekeeping the pewter mug he has won — along with an envelope filled with fifty ten-dollar bills, of which Sharif, who rightly considers himself the Rod Laver of American squash, is somewhat contemptuous. "I wonder," he asks, "how many thousands of dollars that dinner and all those drinks cost last night?"

Hashim, with the cup tucked under one arm and the long narrow bag that squash and tennis players carry in the other, makes his way across the room toward the door. He is still limping slightly, and I am reminded that Hashim did not come to this Open tournament just to watch his son win or to coach his nephew or to carry back the loot. He has come as one of the sixteen competitors, as he has come to all but one of the North American Open tournaments since its inception in 1954. This year in the first round he met twenty-seven-

year-old John Reese, the number one ranked American amateur of the 1971 season. Hashim won the first two games easily, 15-8, 15-10. Then toward the end of the third, he made a sudden change of direction and wrenched his knee. After losing the point, he had a look at the leg, examining it coolly, as if it were a piece of faulty machinery, bending the knee this way and that to see where the trouble lay. Evidently deciding that it was serviceable, he went on and won the game at 15-9 and the match. But the next morning the knee was so swollen and sore that Hashim was forced to default to Larry O'Loughlin. And lest one suppose that it is a fluke that this fifty-five- or sixty-year-old man can beat one of the best young amateur players, let it be noted that in the quarter-finals of last year's Open, Hashim eliminated twenty-three-year-old Anil Nayar, the former champion of India and the reigning U.S. amateur champion. But for that performance he required four games. Then in the semi-finals Sharif beat his father, and then took his cousin Mohibullah in the finals.

Khans, Khans, Khans. The name must give aspiring champions nightmares. It has been five years since anyone not named Khan has triumphed in the North American Open, and before that one has to go back seven years in the record book to find a different name in the winner's column. Hashim himself has won it four times, Mohibullah five times, and Sharif three times. But what will happen when, sometime in the next five years or so, Sharif, ten pounds heavier and a little less sharp of eye, slumps onto a bench in some club locker room somewhere and sighs, "Well, you can't win them all"?

Plus ça change, plus c'est la même chose. Sharif is only Hashim's oldest squash-playing son. Following Sharif is Gulmast, twenty-two; Aziz, twenty; Laiquat Ali, seventeen; Salim, fourteen; Shaukat Ali, seven; and Mahammed Ali, six. And only Allah knows what will happen if the western atmosphere of Detroit should overcome Hashim's eastern prejudices and he lets the women of his family have a glimpse of the game as he had his first look when he was eight years old back in Peshawar, forty-nine — or is it fifty-four — years ago.

THE RULES

Reproduced courtesy of the United States Squash Racquets Association

Single's Rules – Interpretation and Referee's Guidelines

Official Playing Rules of the United States Squash Racquets Association. Revised.

SINGLES

♦ 1. SERVER

At the start of a match the choice to serve or receive shall be decided by the spin of a racquet. The server retains the serve until he loses a point, in which event he loses the serve.

Rule 1 – Interpretation and Referee's Guidelines

(a) Rule self-explanatory.

(b) The spinning of the racquet almost never requires any supervision by the referee although it is within his control and jurisdiction.

♦ 2. SERVICE

A ball is in play from the moment at which it is delivered in service until

(a) the point is decided;

(b) a Fault, as hereinafter defined, is made; or

(c) a Let or Let Point, as hereinafter defined, occurs.

At the beginning of each game, and each time there is a new server, the ball shall be served from whichever service box the server elects and thereafter alternately until the service is lost or until the end of the game. If the server serves from the wrong box there shall be no penalty and the service shall count as if served from the correct box, provided, however, that if the receiver does not attempt to return the service, he may demand that it be served from the other box, or if before the receiver attempts to return the service, the referee calls a Let, as hereinafter defined, the Service shall be made from the other box.

The server, until the ball has left the racquet from the service, must stand with at least one foot on the floor within, and not touching the line surrounding the service box and serve the ball onto the front wall above the service line and below the 16′ line before it touches any other part of the court, so that on its rebound (return) it first strikes the floor within, but not touching, the lines of the opposite service court, either before or after touching any other wall or walls within the court. A ball so served is a good service, otherwise it is a Fault.

If the first service is a Fault, the server shall serve again from the same side. If the server makes two consecutive Faults, he loses the point. A service called a Fault may not be played, but the receiver may volley any service which has struck the front wall in accordance with this rule.

Rule 2 – Interpretations and Referee's Guidelines

1. "Delivered in service" means any attempt to serve the ball by tossing it up and striking at it. A ball which is tossed up without striking at it has not been delivered in service.

2. The recitation "shall be served" indicates that a referee should direct the server to the correct box. This may be done by specifying the box side before each point or, preferably, by merely correcting the choice of the player whenever he chooses the wrong box. If a serve is made from the wrong box and the point played to completion, service court thereafter is alternated. If the first service is a fault, then the second serving must be from the same box.

3. The recitation "one foot on the floor within" means that at least one foot must be wholly within the quarter circle not touching the line from the time the server takes his stance until the time the ball is contacted by the racquet.

4. A referee shall call a let to prevent any "quick" service before the receiver is prepared. Once the ball has been served a player may not thereafter receive a let on the grounds of any change in his physical condition, such as something in his eye, or because of any defect in his attire or equipment, such as fogged glasses.

5. A referee shall be alert for a reverse service which, instead of being hit directly cross court, is hit on the front wall close to the same side wall as the serving box so as to rebound off the same side wall and cross court. This serve may be hit so close to the corner as to have almost the same trajectory whether it hits the front wall first, as it must to be a good serve, or hits the side wall first as a fault.

6. If the striker attempts to volley the service and misses completely, he may nonetheless make a good return on a successive attempt *if* the ball is a good serve. In this situation, the server may be trapped between the striker and the front wall on the second swing such that the

provisions of Rules 8b and 9b may be applicable. Sometimes the ball missed on the first swing will land outside the service area and be a fault.

7. The ceiling and lights are out-of-court (Rule 3d). Any space below the ceiling above the sixteen foot out-of-court lines is in play and not out-of-court. In some courts lights protrude some distance from the ceiling into the playing area. Local rules may prevail, but the rule should be decided upon and announced prior to start of play. Also in some courts ventiliating ducts or screens may be located in one or more of the court walls below the out-of-court line. Again, local rules may prevail. Door cracks, handles, or peepholes may cause bad bounces. Local rules may allow the referee to award a let under these circumstances.

8. The most difficult fault calls for a referee are usually on hard services close to the front wall service line. One thing to watch for in calling services is whether there is white wall space between the line and the ball. It is better to focus on the front wall service line with a hard serve rather than trying to follow the flight of the ball from the racquet of the server. The fault should be called quickly and loudly by simply saying "fault". On hard serves, the judgeless referee must pay more attention to line faults than to foot faults because of the difficulty of watching the foot at the instant the ball is struck and then shifting his eyes to the front wall to observe line faults. Even a judgeless referee can usually detect most foot faults by noting the position of the foot at the beginning of the service and then shifting focus just before service. Because of the difficulty with line faults and foot faults, it is common practice to have either judge c-ll foot faults, in which case the judge calls out "foot fault" quickly and loudly when he sees it. The referee will immediately call fault, or foot fault, on any service he believes to be bad whether a judge calls it or not. Of course during play after service, the referee makes all calls.

◆ 3. RETURN OF SERVICE AND SUBSEQUENT PLAY

(a) To make a good return of a service or of a subsequent return the ball must be struck on the volley or before it has touched the floor twice, and reach the front wall on the fly above the tell-tale, and it may touch any wall or walls within the court before or after reaching the front wall. A return is deemed to be made at the instant the ball touches the racquet of the player making the return.

(b) If the receiver fails to make a good return of a good service, the server wins the point. If the receiver makes a good return of service the players shall alternate making returns until one player fails to make a good return. The player failing to make a good return loses the point.

(c) Until the ball has been touched or has hit the floor twice, it may be struck at any number of times.

(d) If at any time the ball hits outside the playing surfaces of the court, which includes the ceiling and/or lights or hits a line marking the playing surfaces of the court (except on the first service, when it is one Fault), it is a point against the player so hitting the ball.

Rule 3 – Interpretation and Referee's Guidelines

In General

There are two common loss-of-point situations where the ball hits the floor twice before being fairly returned. In one situation, after leaving the front wall a good return hits the floor twice before being hit on an attempted return. In the other situation, the ball is struck fairly in an attempt to make a return and the ball does not reach the front wall. Either situation is called "not up". Another common loss-of-point situation is when the ball hits on the ceiling or walls above the upper wall lines. This situation is called "out-of-court". The consistent use of these terms by referees will aid in being understood by players, judges, and gallery. Also, these terms require a minimum of time to state and a minimum of additional explanation by the referee which enables the primary focus of attention to remain on the players where it belongs.

3(a) – A ball may be returned directly to the front wall without touching either side wall or the rear wall. The ball may also be returned indirectly by any combination of side wall and/or back wall rebound including rebound from either side wall or from the back wall, or rebound from both side walls or rebound by any back-wall, side-wall combination.

With a boast shot, a combination of rebounds from opposite side walls which rebounds from the second wall closely adjacent to the front wall, it may be difficult to determine whether the ball hits the front wall because the spin causes it to leave the second side wall almost parallel to the front wall. Watch for a change in direction caused by contact with and rebound from the front wall. Usually, the reaction of the ball will indicate whether or not it is up.

It should be noted that a "return is deemed to be made at the instant the ball touches the racquet of the player making the return." Thus, a double hit which sometimes occurs close to the side walls is precluded as is any second attempt in the event that the ball merely grazes the racquet and the player could otherwise hit a good shot on a second attempt.

The ball may be fairly hit by any part of the racquet, including the handle and frame. Sometimes a ball hitting first on the strings closely adjacent the frame will hit the frame after leaving the strings. Sometimes a ball hitting first on the frame will then hit the strings. In each situation the return is bad and the point is lost.

A ball may not be carried on the racquet and must rebound directly and immediately from the racquet upon being struck.

3(b),(c),(d) – If a service or other shot is "not up" or "out of court," a player cannot make it good by playing it or attempting to play it.

◆ 4. SCORE

Each point won by a player shall add one to his score.

Rule 4 – Interpretations and Referee's Guidelines

The score shall be announced after each point. The referee or marker (separate scorer) shall announce first the score of the player who won the point, and who is therefore serving the next point; and second the score of the player who lost the point, and who is therefore receiving. "Zero" is "love", as in most racquet games.

The announcement of the score is primarily for the benefit of the players and secondarily for the benefit of the gallery. The announcement should be made loudly and clearly. There is usually no need to announce who won the point other than by the aforementioned custom of announcing first the score of the player winning the preceding point since it will usually be obvious to both the players and gallery who won the point anyway. If the winner of the point is not obvious, it is often a good idea to announce who won the point so that there will be no misunderstanding on the part of the players. Whoever is keeping score should be attentive to the noise level and the readiness of the players to proceed. Usually, with a knowledgable and appreciative gallery, the scorer waits for the applause to subside before announcing the score. However, if the players are ready to play before the noise subsides, the scorer announces the score immediately so as not to interfere with play.

◆ 5. GAME

The player who first scores fifteen points wins the game excepting that:

  (a) At "thirteen all" the player who has first reached the score of "thirteen" must elect one of the following before the next serve:
    (1) Set to five points—making the game eighteen points.
    (2) Set to three points—making the game sixteen points.
    (3) No set, in which event the game remains fifteen points.

  (b) At "fourteen all" provided the score has not been "thirteen all" the player who has first reached the score of "fourteen" must elect one of the following before the next serve:
    (1) Set to three—making the game seventeen points.
    (2) No set, in which event the game remains fifteen points.

◆ 6. MATCH

A match shall be best three out of five games.

Rules 5 and 6 – Interpretations and Referee's Guidelines

When the game is set to 3, 5, or no set, the referee should announce "no set", "set 3", or "set 5". Thereafter the scorer should give the game score as before if "no set" is chosen but, if a "set 3" or "set 5" is chosen, the scorer should then give a "set" score, e.g. "2-1, set 3"

When game or match point is reached, there is no need for the score keeper to make any special announcement of that fact since most certainly the players and probably everyone else will know what the situation is.

Upon completion of a game point or match point, it is appropriate to announce: "Game, Mr. Jones" or "Game-match, Mr. Jones", or the like. After the completion of a game and before completion of the match and after the applause has subsided, it is appropriate to announce the game and match score to the gallery, as by "Mr. Jones won the second game 15-11, games stand 1 all."

Prior to the start of the fourth game, the referee or scorer should announce the game score: "Mr. Jones leads 2 games to 1 and will serve."

◆ 7. KEEP OUT OF OPPONENT'S WAY

Each player must get out of his opponent's way immediately after he has struck the ball and

  (a) Must give his opponent a fair view of the ball, provided, however, interference purely with his opponent's vision in following the flight of the ball is not a Let;

  (b) Must give his opponent a fair opportunity to get to and/or strike at the ball in any position on the court elected by his opponent;

  (c) Must allow his opponent to play the ball from any parts of the court elected by his opponent; and

  (d) Must allow his opponent to play the ball to any part of the front wall or to either side near the front wall.

Rule 7 – Interpretations and Referee's Guidelines

In General

This is perhaps the most important rule in squash and probably the one causing the most controversy in a match when a let is requested for violation thereof. The key words are *"must* get out of his opponent's way *immediately* after he has struck the ball." Violation of this rule is in no way related to intent or mistake. An attempt to clear is not sufficient. Inadvertence is no excuse nor is being too slow or too tired. A let should be granted in any situation where the striker could have gotten to and struck at the ball except for the physical presence in the court of the opponent. The location of the ball and the players is immaterial. The only question is whether, at the time the let situation occurs, the player interfered with could have gotten to and struck at the ball before the point would have otherwise been terminated. While Rule 9 provides for the evaluation of the likelihood of the player having been able to make a return, the question is could he reasonably have attempted a return and would he have been able to return the shot fairly. Whether the return would have been good or not is of no concern. Going the wrong way is not necessarily grounds for denial of a let. Attempting to play the ball in an unorthodox manner is not necessarily grounds for denial of a let. The making of a good shot by a player is not grounds for denial of a let *unless* the shot was irretrievable regardless of the interference, e.g., a dead nick or crack.

7(a) – If there is no actual or prospective physical interference and no intentional obstruction of view, then the mere temporary presence of the player between the ball and his opponent is not grounds for a let. If a player makes an insufficient attempt to clear an obscured shot which is coming toward him or to clear an obscured shot in front of him, a let may be granted if the player's presence prevents his opponent from seeing the ball in time to make an attempt to reach it or strike at it.

7(b)(c) – The striker is entitled to play the ball in any manner from any part of the court. Perhaps the two most common violations of these provisions are "crowding" and "obstruction". In the crowding or obstruction situations, the player moves or stands so close to the striker that he cannot get set to hit or properly stroke the ball. The striker is entitled to enough room to employ a reasonable length back swing and follow through. On the other hand, the striker is not entitled to an unreasonable length follow through. In such a situation, a player hit on the follow through may be entitled to a let or let point if the length of the follow through is unreasonable. The striker may be entitled to a let or let point if the length of the follow through is reasonable and the opponent was crowding or obstructing him.

7(d) – The playing area which a player must clear on each shot varies depending on the position of the ball at the time the opponent elects to strike it. The clear playing area is a variable triangle with a moving apex at the position of the ball and a base extending across the entire front wall and a small part (i.e. about one foot) of the side walls adjacent thereto. Since the triangle of clear playing area varies as the position of the ball changes, a player must watch the ball and his opponent and move accordingly so as to stay out of the clear playing area triangle. Any player who habitually stands on the "T" at the intersection of the service court lines, regardless of the position of the ball and his opponent, may be in the playing area triangle and in violation of Rule 7(d). Under Rule 8(b), any ball going directly to the front wall which hits the player is a point. This penalty may not be adequate because the "blocker" will tend to cause his opponent to play around him and to unfairly obtain controlling positions. Thus, a referee must be fully aware of this problem and the application of Rules 7 and 9, to prevent the situations from developing or being exploited.

In this connection, a player will sometimes be trapped by an unorthodox maneuver or missed shot by his opponent as when an apparent backhand shot is played as a turning forehand or when a swing is a complete miss. In this situation, if the player was out of the apparent clear playing area until there was a sudden and unexpected change in position, he nevertheless loses the point if hit by the ball Rule 8(b), unless the provisions of Rule 9(b) should apply. Of course, the player striking or missing the ball in these situations may be entitled to the full benefit of Rule 7 and may be entitled to a let under the provisions of Rule 8(c) or Rule 9(a) or (c).

◆ 8. BALL IN PLAY TOUCHING PLAYER

If a ball in play, after hitting the front wall, but before being returned again, shall touch either player, or anything he wears or carries (other than the racquet of the player who makes the return) the player so touched loses the point, except as provided in Rule 9(b).

If a ball in play touches the player who last returned it or anything he wears or carries before it hits the front wall, the player so touched loses the point.

If a ball in play, after being struck by a player on a return, hits the player's opponent or anything his opponent wears or carries before reaching the front wall:

(a) The player who made the return shall lose the point if the return would not have been good.

(b) The player who made the return shall win the point if the ball would have gone directly from the racquet of the player making the return to the front wall without first touching any other wall.

(c) The point shall be replayed as a Let (See Rule 9) if the return except for such interference would have hit the front wall fairly and (1) would have touched some other wall before so hitting the front wall, or (2) has hit some other wall before hitting the player's opponent or anything he wears or carries.

When there is no referee, if the player who made the return does not concede that the return would not have been good, or, alternatively, if the player's opponent does not concede that the ball has hit him (or anything he wears or carries) and would have gone directly to the front wall without first touching any other wall, the point shall be replayed as a Let. (See Rule 9).

In all cases covered by this Rule play shall cease even though the ball goes up.

Rule 8 – Interpretations and Referee's Guidelines

The basic premise of this rule is that a player must not unnecessarily interfere with his opponent's right to hit the ball from any part of the court to any part of the front wall or side wall closely adjacent thereto. When the rule is violated by a player being hit with his own shot, he loses the point (unless the provisions of Rule 9(b) apply), because he prevents his opponent from attempting a shot. It may be noted that for the purposes of this rule, the clear playing area is reduced somewhat by including only the front wall and excluding the side wall immediately adjacent thereto. If the player is in the reduced clear playing area when hit by the ball, he is in violation of Rule 7(d) and the penalty is loss of the point. On the other hand, if the player is outside the reduced clear playing area when hit by a ball, which would have been otherwise good, he is not penalized and the point is played over as a Let under Rule 8(c).

The provision of "other than the racquet of the player who makes the return" of course means the *subsequent* return.

Sometimes the ball may nick the clothes worn by the player or a towel carried by him without his knowledge. It is a dead ball at that point and the provisions of Rule 8 apply. If the referee observes the contact, he will immediately stop play and make a ruling. If the referee does not stop play, a player must assume that the referee did not see the contact and keep on playing until the point is otherwise decided, as in the case of a broken ball — for if the player stops play, the referee will have to hold against him unless there are judges who did see the contact and overrule the referee.

Section 8(a) provides that a player hit by a ball loses the point only if the return would have been good. On a ball going to the front wall, the height above the floor of the point of contact of the ball with the opponent may be a good indication of whether the ball would have reached the front wall above the 17" high tell-tale. The speed of the ball and/or angle may indicate that it would not reach the front wall directly. In the event of uncertainty, it is better to award a Let rather than a point.

Section 8(b) specifies the penalty of loss of point when a player is hit with a return.

Section 8(c) is based on the premise that a player who is outside of the reduced clear playing area when hit by an opponent's shot should not be penalized. The position of the player outside the reduced clear playing area is determinable under the provisions of Rule 8(c)(1) by the fact that the ball would have hit one of the side walls or the back wall first. Additionally, even if a player is in the clear playing area, he is not penalized by being hit with a rebound shot as specified in Rule 8(c)(2).

Regardless of what else happens to a shot which has hit a player, play terminates at the moment of contact. It is noted that in club play outside of tournament type competition many players play Let in all situations covered by this rule. Because of this practice, some players have come to believe that an "automatic" Let occurs whenever a player is hit by the ball. On the contrary, there are a number of situations where a Let is not justified and a point should be awarded either for or against the hit player.

Referees and judges must remember that a player who is hit with the ball may win the point if the ball would not have reached the front wall, e.g. been too low or not had sufficient forward momentum.

On a ball headed for the front wall side wall crack, a Let ball shall be awarded.

◆ 9. LET

A Let is the stopping of play and the playing over of a point.

In addition to the Lets described in Rules No. 2 and No. 8 (c), the following are Lets if the player whose turn it is to strike the ball could otherwise have made a good return:

(a) When such player's opponent violates Rule 7;

(b) When owing to the position of such player, his opponent is unable to avoid being touched by the ball;

(c) When such player refrains from striking at the ball because of a reasonable fear of injuring his opponent;

(d) When such player before actually hitting or in the act of striking or striking at the ball is touched by his opponent, his racquet or anything he wears or carries;

(e) When on the first bounce from the floor the ball hits on or above the six and one-half foot line on the back wall; and

(f) When a ball in play breaks. If a player thinks the ball has broken while play is in progress he must nevertheless complete the point and then immediately request a Let, giving the ball to the referee for inspection. The referee shall allow a Let only upon such immediate request if the ball proves in fact to be broken.

A player may request a Let or a Let Point. A request by a player for a Let shall automatically include a request for a Let Point. Upon such request, the referee shall allow a Let, Let Point, or No Let.

No Let shall be allowed on any stroke a player makes unless he requests such Let before actually hitting or in the act of striking or striking at the ball.

The referee may not call or allow a Let as defined in this Rule 9 unless such Let is requested by a player; provided, however, the referee may call a Let at any time (1) when there is interference with play caused by any factor beyond the control of the players, or (2) when he fears that a player is about to suffer severe physical injury.

On the replay of the point the server (1) is entitled to two serves even though a Fault was called on the original point, (2) must serve from the correct box even though he served from the wrong box on the original point, and (3) provided he is a new server, may serve from a service box other than the one he selected on the original point.

Rule 9 – Interpretations and Referee's Guidelines

The very first words of this rule – "Let is the stopping of play and the playing over of a point", are crucial to a correct understanding and application of the provisions thereof. The primary purpose of the Let is to allow the replay of any point on which there is interference caused by an opponent which prevents a player from reaching and/or striking at the ball. Such interference creates Let situations which may take many forms. Also, the purpose of the Let is to allow the stopping of play and the replay of any point on which there is outside interference beyond the control of, and not related to the actions of the players, such as the breaking of the ball, opening of the court door, turning off of the lights, or objects falling into the court.

In most player-created Let situations, it is up to the offended player to decide whether to call Let and stop play, or continue play in spite of the Let situation. The referee should not interfere with the game by calling Lets for the players in Let situations except to prevent injury. If an offended player in a Let situation elects to continue play, i.e. does not call Let and stops play in the process of making or attempting his stroke, no Let can thereafter be granted to him because of that Let situation. The basic premise is that a player may think he has an advantage in playing a shot in a Let situation, and he should have the option of attempting the shot *or* calling Let and stopping play, but he does not have the option of attempting the shot and then calling Let only if the shot is missed or badly played.

Since Let is the stopping of play, whenever a Let is called, play is stopped then and there regardless of what subsequently happens to the ball or the players. Nothing that happens after a Let is called, i.e. whether the ball goes up, should be considered in deciding whether to grant a Let. A player who calls Let and stops play assumes the risk of losing the point in the event of an adverse decision. If a player calls for a Let which is denied, the point must be awarded to the other player.

The determination of all Lets in player-created Let situations is based upon a consideration of whether the player requesting the Let "would otherwise have made a good return", but for the interference. This provision is generally interpreted to mean that if a player could have gotten to and struck at the ball, he would have made a good return, i.e. one which would have reached the front wall fairly.

Rule 9(a) specifies that violations of Rule 7 are Lets. Such violations are the most common Let situations and reference should be made to Rule 7 for interpretation and instruction.

Rule 9(b) is often overlooked by the players and the referee. Many players believe that a point is lost whenever the opponent is hit with his own shot. When a player is hit with his own shot when trapped between the side wall and the striker and cannot clear without interfering with the striker, a let should be awarded.

Obviously, the provisions of Rule 9(c) should be liberally construed.

The provisions of Rule 9(d) are supplemental to the provisions of Rule 7 in that it covers some situations which Rule 7 does not. The provisions of Rule 9(d) do not provide for an "automatic" let. A player must also comply with the other requirements of Rule 9, such as the requirement that "he requests such Let before actually hitting or in the act of striking or striking at the ball."

Rule 9(e) required no comment.

Rule 9(f) is most often violated by failure of a player to complete the point before requesting Let for a broken ball. The reason why the point should be completed is that a call of Let before completion of the point may stop play with an unbroken ball. A player who calls Let for a broken ball can receive no Let and loses the point if the ball is unbroken. Upon completion of the point, the ball must be given to the referee immediately without testing by the player which might result in causing breakage of an unbroken ball. A broken ball is one that has defect which has visably effected play. An unbroken ball may be removed from the game and replaced by another ball at any time by agreement of the players or decision of the referee, with the point standing as played.

♦ 10. LET POINT

A Let Point is the unnecessary violation of Rule 7 (b), 7 (c) or 7 (d). An unnecessary violation occurs (1) when the player fails to make the necessary effort within the scope of his normal ability to avoid the violation, thereby depriving his opponent of a clear opportunity to attempt a winning shot, or (2) when the player has repeatedly failed to make the necessary effort within the scope of his normal ability to avoid similar violations. The player unnecessarily violating Rule 7 (b), 7 (c) or 7 (d) loses the point.

When there is no referee, if a player does not concede that he has unnecessarily violated Rule 7(b), 7(c), or 7(d), the point shall be replayed as a Let.

Rule 10 – Interpretations and Referee's Guidelines

The primary purpose of the let point is to compensate a player for loss of the opportunity to make a winning point and secondarily to penalize a player who violates the provisions of Rules 7(b), (c), or (d). The key word is "unnecessary". which is to be clearly distinquished from such words as "willful" or "intentional", but which is interpreted to be akin to "unavoidable", as qualified by the definition of unnecessary violation in the Rule. Any player-created Let situation under Rules 7(b), (c), or (d) is a potential let point, if the offending player did not *"make the necessary* effort within the scope of his *normal ability* to avoid the violation." The rule indicates that any failure "to avoid the violation" because of an insufficient effort to comply with Rules 7(b), (c), or (d), which could have been avoided by the offending player, if he had made an effort to do so within the scope of his normal ability, is a potential let point. The fact that a player is tired or injured or slips or makes an error or mistake in judgment is no excuse.

A potential let point under the provisions of Rule 10(a) becomes a let point when the offended player would otherwise have had a *clear opportunity to attempt a winning* shot. The purpose of this provision is to enable the penalty to be fitted to the serverity of the violation, since potential let point situations may range from interference with a center fore-court set up to a scramble in one of the rear corners. The offending player may be hopelessly trapped in the corner or he may have good center court position on the fringe of the clear playing area. Thus, the referee must evaluate each potential let point situation in terms of the positions and actions of the players and the position and action of the ball.

Under Rule 10(b) the penalty aspects of the let point are covered. Typical situations which are within the scope of this rule include habitual or repeated blocking, i.e. failure to clear, and habitual or repeated crowding, i.e. standing or moving in too close to the striker. It is necessary that the referee warn the offending player, no more than once, that such repeated offenses will result in the granting of let points.

Rule 9 provides that any request for let automatically includes a request for let point. If the referee thinks that a let point occurred, he must call "let point". If the referee calls "let", the offended player may specifically ask for a let point or he may appeal. The referee should not be reluctant to call a let point in the proper situation.

♦ 11. CONTINUITY OF PLAY

Play shall be continuous from the first service of each game until the game is concluded. Between each game, play may be suspended by either player for a period not to exceed two-minutes, and between the third and fourth games play may be suspended by either player for a period not to exceed five minutes. Except during the five-minute period at the end of the third game, no player may leave the court without the permission of the referee. The referee may suspend play for such period as he may consider necessary. If play is suspended by the referee because of an injury to one of the players, such player must resume play within one hour or default the match. The foregoing provisions shall be strictly construed. Play shall never be suspended to allow a player to recover his strength or his wind. The referee shall be the sole judge of intentional delay, and, after giving due warning, he must disqualify the offender.

In the event the referee suspends play other than for injury to a player and for some cause beyond the control of both players, such as the failure of the electric lighting system, play shall be resumed when the cause of such suspension of play has been eliminated, provided, however, if such cause of delay cannot be rectified within one hour, the match shall be postponed to such time as the Tournament Committee determines and the match shall be resumed from the point and game score existing at the time the match was stopped unless the referee and both players unanimously agree to play the entire match or any part of it over.

Rule 11 – Interpretations and Referee's Guidelines

The referee should enforce the provisions of this rule regarding rest periods by timing the rest period between games and by requesting the players to play upon completion of the rest period. Since the rule contemplates that play be resumed at the end of the rest period, the referee should warn the players of the impending termination of the period so that they may be ready at the end of the period. During the two (2) minute period, the referee should announce "15 seconds" at the 1:45 minute mark. During the five (5) minute period, the referee should announce the "1 minute" at the 4:00 minute mark and should have notice taken to any player who has left the court and not returned. Similarly, the referee should enforce the provisions of the rule regarding continuity by requesting any player in violation of the rule to continue without further delay. If one player is in position and ready to play, the referee can force the play by simply calling "play"

If a player attempts to leave the court at any time other than between the third and fourth games, the referee should remind him that he may not do so without permission. The referee should allow a player to leave the court between games for any legitimate reason not involving an attempt to or resulting in delay of the game or extension of the rest period.

The most common forms of delay involve the use of towels and/or the cleaning of glasses. There is no provision in the rules for the stopping of play for these purposes. However, if the amount of delay is not unreasonable and the use of the towel does not appear to be resorted to merely for purposes of delay, then the referee should not prevent it.

♦ 12. ATTIRE AND EQUIPMENT

(a) Player's attire must be white. Any controversy over attire shall be decided by the referee, whose decision shall be final.

(b) The standard singles ball of the United States Squash Racquets Association shall be of black rubber 1.700 to 1.750 inches in diameter and shall weigh 1.12 to 1.17 ounces. It shall be pneumatic. At a ball temperature of 70 to 74 degrees Fahrenheit, it shall have a rebound on a steel plate between 24 to 26 inches

from a drop of 100 inches. After ten minutes or more of play or at a ball temperature of 83 to 84 degrees Fahrenheit, it shall have a rebound on a steel plate of 27 to 30 inches from a drop of 100 inches. For a supplementary test in a court, after ten minutes or more of play the ball shall have a rebound from the 6'6" rear red line of not more than 25 inches and not less than 23 inches.

The difference in rebound between a ball before play and after play of ten minutes or more, whatever the temperature of the court or the ball, shall not exceed 20% of the before play rebound.

For purposes of this rule a minimum of 300 blows by the authorized testing device of the Association shall be deemed to be the equivalent of the ten minutes or more of play referred to above, since this procedure yields a ball temperature of 83 to 84 degrees Fahrenheit.

Manufacturers may use the testing device of the Association which is available through the chairman of the Committee on Courts, Bats and Balls or procure their own.

(c) The racquet or bat shall be made of wood and have a circular shaped head with a diameter not exceeding 9 inches, and shall not exceed 27 inches overall length, with a weight of approximately 10 ounces. It shall be strung with gut or a substitute material, provided it is not metal. Materials or racquet designs which do not conform with this section, or the generally recognized manufacturer's standards, should be submitted to the Executive Committee for approval prior to manufacture or usage.

Rule 12 – Interpretations and Referee's Guidelines

The basic reason for the provision of white attire is that the black squash ball is seen best against a white background. Usually, an off-white is not objectionable.

If a player appears in the court for a match in improper attire, the referee shall ask the offending player to change before the match starts. If a player thinks that his opponent's attire is unacceptable, he shall appeal to the referee.

♦ 13. CONDITION OF BALL

(a) No ball, before or during a match, may be artificially treated—that is, heated or chilled.

(b) At any time, when not in actual play, another ball may be substituted by the mutual consent of the contestants or by decision of the referee.

Rule 13 – Interpretations and Referee's Guidelines

The ball should be brought to playing temperature only by stroking it with the racquet in the court.

♦ **14. CONDITION OF COURT**

No equipment of any sort shall be permitted to remain in the court during a match other than the ball used in play, the racquets used by the players, and the clothes worn by them. All other equipment, such as extra balls, extra racquets, sweaters when not being worn, towels, bathrobes, etc., must be left outside the court. A player who requires a towel or cloth to wipe his eyeglasses should keep same in his pocket or securely fastened to his belt or waist.

Rule 14 – Interpretations and Referee's Guidelines

The reason for keeping extra clothing and equipment out of the court is to prevent any interference with play which might come about by stepping thereon or by being hit by the ball or by distracting a player. Also, the game ball might inadvertently get mixed up with an extra ball or balls.

♦ **15. REFEREE**

(a) A referee shall control the game. This control shall be exercised from the time the players enter the court. The referee may limit the time of the warm-up period to five minutes, or shall terminate a longer warm-up period so that the match commences at the scheduled time. The referee's decision on all questions of play shall be final except as provided in Rule 15(b).

(b) Two judges may be appointed to act on any appeal by a player to a decision of the referee. When such judges are acting in a match, a player may appeal any decision of the referee to the judges, except as provided in paragraph (d) hereof. If one judge agrees with the referee, the referee's decision stands; if both judges disagree with the referee, the judges' decision is final. The judges shall make no rulings unless an appeal has been made. The decision of the judges shall be announced promptly by the referee.

(c) A player shall not state his reasons for his request under Rule 9 for a Let or Let Point or for his appeal from any decision of the referee or judges, provided, however, that the referee may request the player to state his reasons.

(d) After giving due warning, the referee in his discretion may disqualify a player for speech or conduct unbecoming to the game of squash racquets. This decision of the referee may not be appealed.

Rule 15 – Interpretations and Referee's Guidelines

The current generally accepted theory of refereeing is that the game belongs to the players and that the referee *should not* interfere with the playing of any point unless to prevent injury or in the event of outside interference. The function of the referee essentially should be to indicate the termination of play or completion of a point, and to render decisions when asked to do so by one or both of the players. However, commencing with the five (5) minute warning period, the referee has complete power over the match and should exercise that power to control the match, including the conduct of the players and the gallery whenever it is necessary to do so in the best interests of the game.

The referee should not interject his personality into the game nor detract from the focus of attention of the gallery on the game. Nonetheless, the referee should attempt to keep the gallery informed of the score and of all decisions.

In connection with indicating the termination of play or completion of a point, the referee should strive to make and announce his decision quickly. To a great extent, the referee should be able to rely on the judgment of the players with respect to gets and returns. Many players will signal by raising their hand whenever they think that a ball was not up. Also, most players will terminate play when they think they have failed to make a good return so that it is unnecessary for the referee to make any call except to announce the score. Of course, if the referee is convinced the ball is not up, he should make the call before there is any further play. In connection with out-of-court calls as with fault calls which are essentially line determinations, the referee should call "out of court" or "fault" immediately.

The referee must give his full attention to the game and shall locate himself in the center of the first row of the gallery. In order to obtain the best possible view of the action, the referee will often have to move about at his vantage point, shifting from side to side or standing or leaning forward to see the ball along the back wall. If the referee thinks of himself as a third player, trying to reach and return every shot, he will be "in the game" and his concentration will equal that of the players.

In the event that a player asks for a decision by the referee on a particular matter, the referee should first be sure that he understands what matter is under consideration, and if he is not sure, should ask the player for clarification. However, if the player thinks that the matter in controversy may not have been observable by the referee, and the referee does not ask for clarification, a short statement of the basis of the request may be permissible. Unless the referee asks for clarification, the player should not be permitted to argue the point. The referee must render a judgment.

Whether the referee actually saw the event is immaterial. The referee, as well as the judges, must give his best judgment on the basis of what he can infer from what he could observe. The referee should give his decision without a supporting opinion by simply stating "let" or "no let" or whatever. If the player questions an out-of-court, not up type call (or the lack of it), the decision of the referee has already been rendered directly or indirectly, and the referee should merely confirm that decision by a simple statement such as "I thought it was good (or out or down), but you may appeal."

If the player elects to appeal, it should be made clear to the judges, if necessary, what decision is being appealed. If a judge supports the referee's decision, the appeal is denied without reference to the other judge. If the first judge disagrees with the referee's decision, then the referee must ask for the decision of the other judge. The result of the appeal should be announced to both the players and the gallery by a simple statement such as "referee sustained" or "referee overruled".

Index